THE DOER OF GOOD
BECOMES GOOD

A Primer on Volunteerism

Ronald W. Poplau

ScarecrowEducation
Lanham, Maryland • Toronto • Oxford
2004

Published in the United States of America
by ScarecrowEducation
An imprint of The Rowman & Littlefield Publishing Group, Inc.
4501 Forbes Boulevard, Suite 200, Lanham, Maryland 20706
www.scarecroweducation.com

PO Box 317
Oxford
OX2 9RU, UK

British Library Cataloguing in Publication Information Available

Library of Congress Cataloging-in-Publication Data

Poplau, Ronald W. (Ronald Wayne), 1937–
  The doer of good becomes good : a primer on volunteerism / Ror
Poplau.
    v. cm.
  Includes bibliographical references and index.
  Contents: The three Rs and community service — Soul food for t
inner person — Mechanics of a community service program — Th
of community service on students — Intergenerational service mo(
From Russia with love — The future.
  ISBN 1-57886-082-2 (pbk. : alk. paper)
  1. Student service–United States–Case studies. 2. Student
volunteers in social service–United States–Case studies. [1. Studen
service. 2. Voluntarism.] I. Title.
LC220.5 .P66 2004
361.3'7–dc22   2003019654

⊗™ The paper used in this publication meets the minimum requ
American National Standard for Information Sciences—Permanen
Paper for Printed Library Materials, ANSI/NISO Z39.48-1992.
Manufactured in the United States of America.

This book is dedicated to my dear wife and companion
for over thirty-six years, Linda Poplau: faithful friend,
my strength, and one deeply loved.

"Nothing but what you volunteer has the essence of life, the s
of pleasure in it. These are the things you do because you wan
them, the things that your spirit has chosen for its satisfaction

—Woodrow ٧

CONTENTS

ACKNOWLEDGMENTS

No one writes a book alone. It is a compilation of talents of many people. I am indebted to many individuals too numerous to mention.

To my son, Jim, who edited the manuscript. Without his verbal genius and computer skills, this book would never have been printed.

To my daughter, Kristy, for successfully introducing community service to the inner-city schools, proving beyond a doubt that this program can be implemented anywhere.

To the Scarecrow staff: my debts include Tom Koerner, who accepted my original proposal; Cindy Tursman, for her assistance and directions; Amos, Mary Jo, Andrew, and Mary for their encouragement and professional recommendations.

My special thanks to my beloved Northwest High School: Dr. Harrington's guiding hand and friendship for many years; all of my incredible students who lived this story every day. This is my attempt to let the world know you are the finest young men and women who will change the world for the better.

FOREWORD

Service to the community is one of life's most rewarding experiences. This simple truth has guided me throughout my four-plus decades of volunteering and public service. Commitment to service comprises a major portion of my life as a U.S. Congressman, and I'm honored for the opportunity to introduce Ron Poplau's book.

Ron is a beloved community service teacher at Shawnee Mission Northwest High School, a Blue Ribbon school in my congressional district. He has been inducted into both the National Teachers Hall of Fame and the Mid-America Education Hall of Fame. His class on community service is so popular that enrollment has been capped at an amazing 480 students each school year. The class has won the Kansas Governor's Spirit of Giving Award and the J.C. Penney's Golden Rule Award five times. It was the inspiration for Kansas state legislation requiring community service activities in Kansas schools. Ron has presented his programs in Russia, and the class was featured at an international conference on volunteerism in Istanbul.

I know as a father, and now a grandfather, a parent can have no greater wish than to see their children become successful, happy, and healthy adults. Ron's program, Cougars Community Commitment (CCC), takes a dynamic and far-reaching approach to teaching our kids

about aiding others. He has inspired a generation of young
take action on community issues and initiatives.

The extent of our success is due to others taking the tir
about and serve our individual and community needs. It has
the fundamental debts, like the ones that students owe to the
and parents, can never be paid back. They are too big for tl
must be paid forward to those who will come after us.

Ron's students have demonstrated their understanding o
to "pay it forward" time and time again. It is impossible to
ways our community has been enhanced through the CCC
but a few of the ways they have made a difference include: d
the Visiting Nurses Associated Youth; aiding inner city c
Kansas City; providing Thanksgiving dinner for families in
ticipating in the STARS program to help elementary stuc
homework; sponsoring an Intergenerational Prom for senio
long-term care facilities; sponsoring holiday parties for lc
planning a faculty appreciation breakfast to honor educatoi
teeing a loan so a woman could keep her home; painting th
man who had a heart attack; donating to the New York Fi
fighters; paying for medical expenses for a child living with i
dition; providing Christmas presents for seniors who outlive(
atives; writing letters to military personnel serving ab
assisting low-income persons with delinquent utility bills i
service from being terminated.

Through these efforts and countless others, the stud
learned that community service is not something that happ
point in time and is then over. It is a process that continue:
challenges and new ventures, and its potential is only reache(
is a lifelong experience. For over forty years, Ron has sharec
sons with his students, motivating them to realize their full p
enriching the lives of those around them, as well as their o\
you enjoy reading Ron's heartfelt narrative and take inspir;
the ideas he shares.

Perhaps the greatest gift you could bestow upon your own (
would be to start a program like CCC and begin with the yo
around you on a path that will carry them through the rest of
fostering good works every step of the way. Certainly, the tit

book is as true now as it was when it first appeared in print centuries ago in the Brihadaranyaka Upanishad of the Hindu tradition: "The doer of good becomes good."

Dennis Moore
Congressman, Third District, Kansas

INTRODUCTION

The impossible is often the untried.

—Jim Goodwin

This book was written with a great deal of conviction. I have an axe to grind here. It is razor sharp and will cut through the theory and malaise of education.

One of my former professors referred to me as the "apostle" of volunteerism. My mission is community service. My objective is to have it in all schools, across the nation.

How would you feel if you discovered the cure for cancer? I doubt any of us would hide such a discovery. Imagine how Jonas Salk must have felt discovering the cure for polio. He changed the world forever. The past ten years have been nothing short of miraculous. I want to share my "discovery" with you.

I agree with those who believe that American education is at a crossroads. Something new needs to be applied. Some critics of education believe that when students come to school, they interrupt their education! We could all agree that information outside school has grown to colossal proportions.

This is truly an age of miracles. Technology, breakthroughs in electronics, media advancements, and so forth are causing us to lose the human touch. Consider books such as *The Greening of America, Fut The People Shapers, The Medium Is the Massage.* We were forewarned that our lack of humaneness would be a major by- such scientific advances.

There are ATMs in church lobbies, Web site sermons, prayer groups, and even confessions online. One can even "] watch the Hajj, the Muslim pilgrimage to Mecca, live!

As a former drug resource staff member in our high school privy to numerous crises all too frequently. Students, simply drugs to feel better. How do we achieve the humane-high, t life? As educators, we must make opportunities available to s develop their "bonding" potential, a humane form of curricu development must occur on a daily basis during the school d

This is my forty-second year in education. Education is tl profession, the most creative enterprise anyone can imagine is sacred, and I have no regrets about a single day of my c most productive years, however, have been the past ten when I worked with embarked on a community service adventure.

The class has grown from one period to six during the day. ber of participants went from seventeen to 480. The local pr ferred to this class as the class of miracle workers. The stu won nearly every award possible and even put their teacher tional Teacher's Hall of Fame. Is it any wonder that I am exc

This is not a treatise on education. It may be my first and There is so much to share with you. Please consider beginning into community service, regardless of what level you are teac

As coordinator for the graduate recertification courses at O versity, I am privy to the feelings of thousands of teachers. Tl many reservations in the profession. "Read and recite, tell a "bells and cells" are the death knell of today's education. Onc community service a try, you will be amazed at what a differ on your teaching career.

After you read this book, you will be convinced that regular l students can be capable of raising $24,000, saving a couple home, converting "druggie" students into miracle workers, and ing the aged. Of all places, the country of Russia, which, a threatened to bury us, was asking for "how to" advice regardir nity service. Their goal is to instigate the program in their sch

At Shawnee Mission Northwest High School in Shawnee, Kansas, test scores are up, National Merit Scholars abound, and dropout rates are reduced. The school was given the coveted "Blue Ribbon School" award, as well as being designated a National "School of Service" for the past three years. Visitors have included the governor of Kansas and a congressman who brought a special letter of congratulations from the president himself!

All of this has occurred in the past ten years.

The answers to many questions about community service are right here at your fingertips. I know that many teachers are going to scream "Oh no, not another subject to teach!" Times have changed. Families used to teach their children concern for others. The percentage of families teaching this "humaneness" is too low today.

A philosopher once wrote: "The meaninglessness of life is the neurosis of our age." Community service works and is well worth the time if it is implemented in your school's curriculum. You might say, "We must draw the line somewhere!" In every classroom, there lurks a sleeping giant, who once awakened, knows no rest. The students, after a mere introduction, will carry the torch and turn daily occurrences into modern miracles. I envy you if this is your first step in the direction of community service. You, too, will change along with your students.

Community service is not an academic subject. No matter how hard we try, it cannot be an academic offering on its own. There is no examination in the service classroom—they either do it or they don't! I am not opposed to academics, but education is more than teaching knowledge and skills. I agree with Haim Ginott who references this poignant message from a principal to his staff at the beginning of a school year:

I am a survivor of a concentration camp. My eyes saw what no man should witness: gas chambers built by learned engineers. Infants killed by trained nurses. Women and babies shot and burned by high school and college graduates. So, I am suspicious of education. Help your students become human. Your efforts must never produce learned monsters, skilled psychopaths or educated Eichmanns.

I am grateful to my school district, my high school, and, above all, to each of my students for making community service work. This is a dynamic success story that can be repeated in every school. I encourage you to become involved.

1

THE THREE R'S AND COMMUNITY SERVICE

My brother had always told me about the program and I planned to take it, but nothing prepared me for what I got. This program is uncanny, the effect it has had on me and other people is unmatched and will be forever.

—Joe Carey

Students don't care how much you know until they know how much you care.

Let's pretend that Ben Franklin has returned to Philadelphia today. His first task would be monumental: *orientation.* He would stand in utter bewilderment at the skyscrapers, automobiles, music, airplane travel, and motion pictures! For a moment, let your imagination supply all of the differences between his world and ours. It probably would come as no surprise that the only institution he would recognize would be the school. The layout of the room is still the same. Franklin would recognize the traditional Three Rs: reading, writing, and 'rithmetic.

Education, according to Woodrow Wilson, is simply a preparation for life. From this we could deduce that if life changes, then so should our education. The decision of change rests in the hands of the classroom teacher. Let's examine one example of how someone can affect the lives of students by simply asking them what they need!

A young man began a teaching career in St. Paul, Minnesot
The position, teaching sociology, provided a generous salary
and even a place to live! He accepted the position on a dare
received a Minnesota teaching certificate. It was obvious the
day on the job that he had made a monumental mistake.

Effective teaching is an art! He didn't even know the rudim
art, not having completed a student teaching experience.
memorizing lectures and found problematic student behav
there was none. What he had become was a public spea
teacher. The old adage is true: "You cannot fool all the peo
time!"

An English teacher rescued him from certain failure by b
ing, "Do you know how much your students hate you?" She
enough to add, "But do you know how much they want to lov
morrow, just sit on the desk and ask your students why you
ting along." His immediate response was one of anger and re
How dare this woman intrude into his professional life?!

The next day, the teacher stuttered and stammered, but n
ask the class just why they weren't getting along. All of their h
up! Students suggested guest speakers, field trips and,
amounted to community service. The students left the bu
campaigned for political candidates, toured the state capito
mately became specialists in community service.

People were fed and homes were refurbished. Quiet and u
students were magically transformed into living dynamos! Pa
dumbfounded by their children's zest for school. Grades shot
tendance reached almost perfection. Even the principal w
that a first-year teacher could become one of the most effec
ers in the school—all from following students' advice!

The school board began to question some of the activities o
The students immediately "put the wagons in a circle" to c
teacher and their newfound effective instruction. Learning w
"fun" and meaningful. Little did this teacher know then that
school juniors and seniors would be the forerunners of his
dents of community service. Students need to be a part of th
and execution of any subject matter. The young teacher was
that the "classroom" existed beyond the four walls of a room.

It's kind of fun to do the impossible.

—Walt Disney

We live in an age of technological miracles. Schools have become warehouses for the most sophisticated electronic equipment. With our phone and "cell" technology there is no place in the world where one cannot directly "call" and speak with someone. Our problem in human relations is not "long distance," but "short distance." The unfortunate side effect is a lack of human interaction.

Let's pretend for a moment that God suddenly decided to install an answering machine in heaven. The experience would go something like this:

Thank you for calling heaven.
For English, press one.
For Spanish, press two.
For all other languages, press three.
Please select one of the following options:
Press one for request.
Press two for thanksgiving.
Press three for complaints.
Press four for all others.

I am sorry, all our angels and saints are busy helping other sinners right now. However, your prayer is important to us and we will answer it in the order it was received. Please stay on the line. If you would like to speak to:

God, press one
Jesus, press two
Holy Spirit, press three

To find a loved one who has been assigned to heaven press five, then enter his Social Security number followed by the pound sign.

If you receive a negative response, please hang up and dial area code 666.

For reservations to heaven, enter JOHN followed by the numbers, 316.

Our computers show that you have already been prayed for today, please hang up and call again tomorrow.

The office is now closed for the weekend to observe a religious holiday.

If you are calling after hours and need emergency assistance, pl(
tact your local pastor.

Thank you and have a heavenly day!

Granted, this is a far-fetched example, but it makes a valic
too often we speak to a machine instead of a person. Many of
machine to screen our calls and decide, on that basis, if we wi

Those of us who were around in the 1960s and 1970s rem
hippie movement and the flower children. Young people w
ning to question our institutions, education in particular. Chai
book, *The Greening of America*, became a runaway best se
had hoped our students would understand that America was c
our world was becoming technically advanced while growi
sonal. In our race to the moon, we ceased to be grounded wit
for humaneness. Values that did not have a price tag were eith
completely or reduced in the order of importance. Science
nology became the new "priesthood."

Many of us assumed *2001: A Space Odyssey* was nothing
science fiction. How could computers ever assume a human
and direct our lives? Scott French, in his book, *Just This Once*
for that human direction in technology. He programmed a
named Hal to think like one of the world's best-selling autho

French's book evokes a very strange feeling! What coulc
How about a college degree with only a minimum of human in
Electronic stores are popping up in many areas, making shop
pletely automated. Students who have been socialized by
education are the first to recognize the joy of dealing with
goodness people!

Sociologists tell us that the average student will change
least three times in his or her lifetime. Regardless of which ca
number of careers a student chooses, he or she will still need
with people. Education must somehow be anchored in the
assume a perpetual becoming. Simply put, we have no idea w
ciety will be like even a year from now.

A good example of this occurred in a K-Mart. You can purc
full of items without ever dealing with a salesperson becau:
mated checkout. At the conclusion of your shopping trip

Thank You for Shopping K-Mart, but somehow that sign fails to convince you that the store was grateful for your business. Electronic sensors are no match for the human touch. ATMs are convenient but they also contribute to the impersonalization of our society. Technology can produce added freedom, but it must be "freedom for" not "freedom from."

Robert D. Putnam, in his highly reviewed study of American life titled *Bowling Alone*, demonstrates that there has been a grievous deterioration over the past twenty years in how Americans relate to one another. The reader is urged to examine his study and his endorsement of community service as a potential remedy.

Note the impact of a student's direct contact with an elderly person:

It's so much fun and it really makes me feel good when I get to help other people. There are so many different ways to go about helping. You can take an active role and work with people directly, or you can be in the background with donations and things like that. People really appreciate your help and they ensure you know you have changed their lives. Gina at The Sweet Life tells me every day how beautiful I am and how special I am and how much she loves me. Once she said she wanted to die and it was her time. I said I'd miss her. So she said, "Okay, I'll talk to the big man and keep ticking to see you every day." I am not related to her, I just met her a few months ago and she makes me feel special.

The Supreme happiness in life is the conviction that we are loved.

—Victor Hugo

More than 700 senior citizens have chosen Lakeview Retirement Village to be their final home. Within this state-of-the-art home are many professional people: politicians, authors, teachers, ministers, and lawyers—the wisdom of over 42,000 years of living experience. This question was posed to them: Which is more important to teach our young people—academics or humaneness? Their responses, confidential and anonymous, overwhelmingly chose humaneness as the most important subject matter in our high schools.

The basic element of community service, especially when it is performed daily, is the bonding experience. Jenny (names have been

changed in examples throughout the book to protect identitie
worst inferiority complex. She was persuaded to try her luck a
derby held annually at Lakeview Retirement Village. She b
fishing tackle and was matched with an elderly resident. They
by side at the lakeshore, talking and snacking.

That morning a shy, despondent young lady was sent to
with the hope of bonding to an elderly person and adding s(
to her life. Just before school dismissed that day, Jenny came
the teacher's room shouting, "I caught the first fish and this
my name and phone number and wants me to come bacl
teacher could do was sit back and watch another miracle unfc
grades began to improve in all her classes. She had bonded t(
who added the much-needed value of self-esteem to her life
has become one of our favorite activities. In terms of bonding
greatest need for both individuals.

We could cite numerous examples of the power of the hui
the spoken words of encouragement, and the effects of servi
ers. How is it possible that words alone could cause a junior l
student to end his life in the presence of other students? 1
overweight boy or girl and they will emphatically deny the ti
adage, "Sticks and stones will break my bones, but words will
me!" This boy shot himself during a biology class to escape (
ridicule.

The final psychological autopsy on the Columbine Hi
tragedy concluded that bullying was the major cause for th;
and inhumane massacre. The two young people who initiate
lence almost daily endured the derision, scorn, and mocker
students with disastrous results. They had planned their den
most a year.

A lack of self-esteem can be difficult to notice. Many sti
guise their insecurities very effectively. One such student,]
had his teacher fooled. He had been a favorite: talented, ha:
and quite handsome. He came from an excellent, affluent far
ine the shock when Jerry, in tears, said farewell to his class ;
ted he had been severely depressed since the seventh grade!

The teacher questioned him and refused to believe the an
would lie awake at night and contemplate suicide. Many nighl

tempt to escape his depression, he would put a knife to his wrists. "Every morning before coming to school, my parents would inspect my wrists. If I had any signs of knife marks, that would be the day they would put me in the hospital. Two things [saved my life]. The [community service] class convinced me that other people actually needed me. I also started reading sacred Scripture. Honestly, I'm telling everyone to take the community service class!"

Jerry returned from Baylor University with an almost straight-A average and maintains his self-esteem with continued community service. When asked why he was depressed for so many years, his response was even more surprising: "Don't you see how I walk—it's different than most people. One of my classmates saw it and they all started to make fun of me!"

> All through high school I have been a jerk. I always made fun of others until I came to this class. I see how much I hurt others by being such a jerk. I guess I chose to hurt others because I was hurting so much inside.
>
> —Tom Cheatham, class of 2003

Many of us are fortunate to have met what we call an unforgettable person. Such a person is SuEllen Fried. She published a book with her daughter Paula titled *Bullies and Victims* (1996). Her research should be in every library in this country and part of teacher training in every college. She has been in great demand as a speaker across the country.

Her research indicates that our schools harbor approximately 2.1 million bullies and 2.7 million victims. The National Education Association estimates 160,000 children miss school every day due to the treatment they receive at the hands of other children. Prison research concludes that a great number of those incarcerated were victims of child abuse. About 25 percent of bullies will have criminal records by the time they are thirty. The number one result of daily community service is a drastic increase in a student's self-esteem.

In her latest book, *Bullies: Targets and Witnesses* (2003), SuEllen Fried reports the lack of humane treatment students experience on a daily basis. Suicide among young people has tripled since 1962, making it the third leading killer of people ages ten to twenty-four.

It is no secret that drugs have become a major part of man
lives. Many modern high schools employ teachers to coord
awareness programs. Whenever new drugs come into stud
these teachers are given information on them and their effec
is a common denominator in the many drug cases that are de
was the quest to "feel better" and enhance the feeling of self-\
sad reality is that students will risk their very lives for an hou
"feeling good."

The popular drug, ecstasy, can be fatal. All too often our y
ple are willing to take that chance for a few moments of che
duced feelings! Thousands attend rave parties on weekends i
warehouses, orchestrated by "drug lords" for personal gain
in community service receive praise and approval every day
dren and adults. You can see students return to their b
tears—holding homemade thank-you cards from area e
schools. Is it any wonder the class at one high school has g
17 to 480 students?

The first president of one community service group admitte
stituted community service for her drug habit. Other student:
fided a similar change in their lifestyles. A judge recently se
young lady to a community commitment program during one
version. In many instances, students are getting the love an
there that is denied them at home. Senior citizens have "ado
students and treat them as if they were their own children.

For too long we adults have hidden behind the expressi
do as I do, do as I say! I'm only human and I have needs, t
are great numbers of people who find out a person is a
the junior-senior level and ask, "How can you stand them
young people are begging for adult role models who sin
their talk."

When we look at our society, who makes and pushes the d
makes and distributes the porno films? Who makes the
Adults! This list could go on and on. In fact, it is not uncomn
a high percentage of parents who are incarcerated for nu
fenses. The book/movie *Lord of the Flies* certainly makes a s
for the effects of a lack of adult involvement in the lives of y
ple. We will look at this more closely in chapter 2.

You may be disappointed if you fail, but you are doomed if you don't try.

—Beverly Sills

The ancient Chinese proverb is especially true for today's young people:

If you want happiness . . .
For an hour—take a nap
For a day—go fishing
For a month—get married
For a year—inherit a fortune
For a lifetime—help someone else.

Community service is not like the discovery of a formula. That only leads to a static conclusion. You will find almost immediately that community service is more like the discovery of a direction, a way to go. If you are a beginner, be warned: look for no road signs. You will be challenged like never before. You must map out everything yourself and question all the conclusions that comprise your philosophy of teaching. In short, you will find you must have "faith" in your "faith."

Even at the expense of sounding immodest, you are reading the only book that I know of that explains community service as it was meant to be: a life-changing experience for each student. Teaching philosophies of Madeline Hunter, William Glasser, and even the British Summerhill project have been studied in relation to this program. Multimedia programs, creating original dramas and simulations, are successful, but nothing provides the satisfaction and professional fulfillment in students like community service.

Community service gives the student a compass, sending them into uncharted territory. The "power" is in the hands of the student. Therein lies the significance and value of this program. Almost all that a student has learned will coalesce into that one hour in the community. The schoolhouse door opens. The fledgling student begins to live what he or she has learned. The role of the teacher suddenly switches from a dispenser of knowledge to a facilitator. We teachers are often accustomed to being simply the source and dispenser of knowledge.

Many of us may feel inept in this new procedural role. For those of you who are traditionalists, or the "read and recite, tell and test" instructor,

keep these students in mind. In the long run, they will pick ¿
what it is they want to learn. Reference the essay written b
Marsh in the community comments section of this book. Sh‹
that her true "learning" really started when she came to sevent
community commitment class. In the words of Woodrow Wil:
were the things her spirit had chosen for its satisfaction."

The community service class not only accentuates the indi
also brings a collective energy to an entire building of student:
some examples that document one school's efforts:

1. Family and home classes found women in a retirement
   special recipes and culinary skills. Invitations were sent to i
   retired women to share their skills with our high school cl
2. Shop classes were asked to make ramps to make homes
   to wheelchairs.
3. Art classes made decorations for an intergenerational p
4. Food classes prepared the refreshments for the prom.
5. English classes prepared prom invitations.
6. Photography classes took pictures of the prom couples.
7. History classes kept a written record of the prom proce
8. It was left to the psychology and sociology classes to di
   significance and its ultimate effect on the school as a wl

The school was working together and each student involve
meaning and value of each discipline's contribution. Commur
created a living textbook.

Is it difficult to begin this "journey of the heart"? Very o
teachers and administrators will ask, "Just what do you do all
students are not in the classroom, so what do you do during
After all, the classroom may be a section of the cafeteria whei
"check in" and out. Should you ever have to respond to this
suggest you keep a daily log for documentation. On a randoı
in a school using the community service model, the followin
and activities were listed:

1. Mary called to ask for additional food. She has enough ı
   for a family of six until Friday. The breadwinner of the
   had an accident at work.

2. I had just cashed my Social Security check and left my purse on the bus. I need to pay my rent or the landlord will kick me out. I called Catholic Charities and they will only give me $100. I was referred to you. Can you help me?

3. Do you have any students who can mow my lawn? I am too old to do it and I had a stroke last spring. I have been cited by the city!

4. This is the secretary at Nieman School. We forgot to tell you that we have parent-conferences today and tomorrow. Please don't send any students today. Sorry about the short notice.

5. Would you and maybe a few of your students be willing to speak at the Rotary luncheon next Thursday? The luncheon is at noon and you would start speaking about 12:45 . . . you will be our guests for lunch.

6. Could you please send us some information about your program? We're thinking of adding community service to our curriculum next year.

7. Your kids did a fine job last night. We are so grateful, we don't know what we would have done without them.

8. Do you have some students, maybe three boys, to help me move some furniture? Ever since I had a heart attack, I can't lift anything.

9. This is Congressman Dennis Moore's office. He would like some of your students this Friday afternoon to help him clean a woman's backyard. We had this all set up as you know for last Friday, but it rained.

10. Our school is having a carnival next week on Thursday evening and we sure would like some of your students again this year to help out.

11. We have a working refrigerator that we would like to give to some needy family, but you will have to have a truck to move it. We'd like it to be this week.

12. If I bought the paint, could your students paint my house? I've been cited by the city and they referred me to you.

If this particular program had twice as many students, the program could place every one of them during every school day. In the history of a school's program, not one student has been known to turn away from

human suffering or human need. Likewise, there has never l
dent who was not changed for the better through only a m
community service. The marvelous daily work of students l
kind of floodlight that lights up their instructors. Their good "
given their conductor excellent reviews. In a real sense, tl
story, imperfectly told by their instructor.

If you are on the fence and skeptical about taking the
beginning a community service program, have faith! It v
those teachers who say, "We can't be expected to do one m(
the only response can be that teachers before us have met
of our young people. Now it is our turn to give them what
most. If we do not meet their needs, who will? We are the
fessional that eventually works with everyone in our soci‹
time or another.

There are a variety of community service programs in t
States. You might want to check the mechanics and merits of ‹
create a hybrid of your own. Many schools have visited Sha
sion Northwest in the past ten years, searching for a model t‹

Many teachers argue that the community service program
in affluent schools with college-prep programs. The Cougar
nity Commitment (CCC) has enjoyed a six-year relationship v
inner-city school that maintains an extensive community s‹
gram.

The CCC attempted to share their program with a school ‹
has many of the same affluent qualities of Shawnee Missior
dents in this district were adamantly opposed to anything th‹
of "sharing the wealth." One student even remarked that the
dents were crazy for doing "so much for nothing in return."

Ben Franklin would have quickly assessed our situation.
ever practical, he would have concluded, "I have never seen ‹
tific advances in my life. Unfortunately, I see so few people
uinely care about others. I would suggest community service
this." After all, it is *the Doer of Good that Becomes Good.*

Years of full-time community service attest to miracles. Th
ture filled with success and affection. I hope you, the reader.
in this through community service.

CHAPTER SUMMARY

1. With the growing increase in scientific advancement, there is a growing impersonalization, especially among our young people.
2. Community service will give young students an opportunity to bond with other people, especially the aged.
3. Community service changes the very nature of teaching. The teacher becomes the procedural element in teaching rather than the dispenser of information, and there is much more activity on the part of the students.
4. Every department in school can lend its expertise to a project, such as a prom for the aged.
5. When given the opportunity, students will become actively involved in their education and will insist on an opportunity for community service.
6. It is simply impossible to put a price tag on some educational values, such as humaneness.
7. Students every day attend six or seven unrelated classes with nothing to link them together. Community service can be that binding link and much of what students learn in school can be used in their time in the community.
8. Community service raises students' self-esteem, and they have an opportunity to bond with adults and be successful at whatever project they undertake.
9. The community itself has a high opinion of young people who do community service and it is willing to participate in school activities and projects.
10. Community service is well worth the time and effort it will take to add it to the curriculum, and the effects will be felt in all the classes.

2

SOUL FOOD FOR THE INNER PERSON

Things are best seen in their beginnings.

—Aristotle

We use the word "good" in a variety of ways:

Good job	Good news
Goodbye	Good Lord
Good night	Good grief
Good deal	Good luck
Good time	Good looking

Early in the school year, a special circumstances test (see table 2.1) is given to each student in the community service class. Students' answers remain anonymous, which promotes their honesty. Students are often offended to realize that in all honesty they do not answer all thirty of the scenarios listed on the test with some degree of "goodness."

No student has ever returned a perfect paper. Students have the option to "share" their scores or keep them confidential. Discussion of each item points out the "good" response. Students even come up with circumstances of their own. The final exam at the end of eighteen weeks

Table 2.1. Circumstances Test

1. You buy something at a store. You receive MORE change back than you are
   Would you
   (a) keep it and leave
   (b) give it back to the salesperson

2. A friend of yours works in a store that you frequent. He offers to "give" yo
   expensive merchandise free. There is no possibility that you will be caught. Y
   (a) accept the merchandise
   (b) refuse the merchandise politely

3. You move into an apartment or house. Cable-TV was not disconnected. The
   canceled but never "cut off." Would you
   (a) keep it and say nothing
   (b) call the cable company and remind them to remove it

4. You receive some expensive merchandise in the mail by mistake. Would you
   (a) keep it
   (b) return it

5. You are about to trade in your car for a new model. There is something ser
   with your car but the mechanic does not detect it. It makes your car worth
   you tell the mechanic. Would you
   (a) say nothing
   (b) tell him about it

6. You are away from home on a business trip. Your spouse is not with you. Th
   "requires" you to have sex with him or he will not buy your merchandise. T
   account for your company and a lot of money for you. Would you
   (a) do it and win the account
   (b) refuse and lose the account

7. A friend of yours offers you some stolen merchandise at a very low price: v
   but your cost $50. It is something that you want. Would you
   (a) buy it
   (b) refuse it

8. You are selling your home. Your basement has a serious water leak when it
   will cause potential buyers to "pass up" buying your home or reduce its val
   substantially. Would you inform a buyer of this problem?
   (a) yes
   (b) no

9. You are offered a good job that requires you to work late hours on school
   will result in grades that average C's or below. Pay is $8.50 an hour. Would
   (a) accept
   (b) refuse the job offer

10. There is a major party at the home of one of your friends. You enjoy that pers
    a lot. Your parents ask you to pass it up to help them with something urgent. V
    (a) stay home and help your parents
    (b) go to the party

11. A friend takes an exam early in the morning. You have that same class later
    offers you correct answers to that exam which you will take later. Would y
    (a) refuse the answers
    (b) get as many as possible

12. You find a billfold or purse with over $200 in it. Would you contact the ow
    return the "billfold" with all the money or would you say you found it with
    money in it?

(a) return it with the money in it

(b) return it without the money or even not at all

13. You buy a record or tape and do not like it. Would you return it and lie and say it was defective or keep it because there are supposed to be no returns unless the tape/record is defective?

(a) keep it

(b) return it and lie

14. Your place of employment has many supplies such as pens, paper, a Xerox machine, etc. Would you help yourself to what you want or limit yourself only to what you need for business?

(a) only for business

(b) personal use and take some home or give to others

15. You work in a fast food place or a theater. Would you give food free or "extras" to your friends or admit them free?

(a) yes (free food, etc.)

(b) no

16. Income tax time: you itemize your deductions. You have a 99 percent chance of not being audited. You would or would not cheat to get a generous refund.

(a) not cheat

(b) cheat

17. You sell your automobile. The buyer asks you to state on the bill of sale a much lower price so he won't have to pay so much sales tax. You would

(a) refuse

(b) lie and list a lower price

18. You have an automobile accident. Unless you lie your insurance will not cover your accident, which will then cost you $1,500. You would

(a) tell the truth

(b) lie

19. Your future spouse wants to know if you have had sex with someone else. You have had "several" experiences. Your truthful response might "break" your engagement forever. You would

(a) tell the truth

(b) lie

20. You have high blood pressure or some other disease. You apply for life insurance. You are asked to report any diseases. The truth will result in not getting the policy or perhaps at a much higher cost. You would

(a) lie

(b) tell the truth

21. You have extra money—about $1,200. Someone asks you to contribute $200 to an urgent charitable cause. You would

(a) refuse and keep all your money

(b) contribute to this worthy cause

22. You attend an out-of-state school. Tuition for nonresidents is 300 percent higher—$122 per credit vs. $42 per credit. A friend offers you a local address you can use so you won't have to pay out-of-state tuition. You would

(a) accept the address

(b) refuse the offer and pay more

23. You order an item from Sears. YOU break it when you open the package at home. Would you return it and say it came that way or pay for a repair?

(continued)

Table 2.1.   Circumstances Test (continued)

    (a) lie about how it "arrived"
    (b) pay for a repair
24. You take your family to a restaurant for a meal. Children under 12 are half |
    your three children are 14 and 15 but look much younger than their age. W
    (a) order all adult meals
    (b) lie about your two children's ages
25. Someone is having an affair with one of your neighbors. Would you express
    disapproval to either of the two people whom you know quite well?
    (a) yes
    (b) no
26. You apply for health insurance. The agent asks you if you smoke or drink. Yc
    reply to either will result in a much higher premium. Would you
    (a) lie and get a lower premium
    (b) admit you smoke or drink
27. Your job pays you by the hour. Would you
    (a) work at a good rate and get paid less
    (b) slow up for more money
28. Your best friend asks you to lie so he/she will either not go to jail or will n
    a large fine. Would you
    (a) tell the truth
    (b) lie to help your friend
29. Your spouse or friend wants to know if you arrived safely at your destinatic
    call person-to-person collect and ask for yourself and save long-distance co
    you
    (a) pay for a legitimate phone call
    (b) call and ask for yourself and save the cost of the call
30. Your child asks you to write a fake note to school so he/she has an excuse
    Your fake note will save your child some serious consequences that will res
    deliberate truancy. Would you
    (a) write a fake note
    (b) not write a note and let your child take the consequences for truancy

of class asks two questions: "Are you now a better person thar eighteen weeks ago? What impact has this class had on your

After establishing the "goodness" quotient of the class, it is that the class define its philosophy of community service. Ta amines the views of five philosophers who have researched a much about the nature of man. Students use the table wher viewpoints regarding community service. Based on these id mission statement is created.

If all five of these philosophers do not provide a workable community service, where do we turn? We can begin with th one does not have to teach a child to be "bad." Good parenting viously alert us to the rights of others. Many times we have Golden Rule, "Do unto others as you would have them do ur

Table 2.2.   Philosopher's Theories

Philosopher	Significance	Philosophy	Problem	Viewpoint
John Locke	Influenced Declaration of Independence "Government is best which governs the least"	People are intrinsically good and need only procedural guidance and control	This position offers no explanation for the obvious evil that exists in the world	Negative: Community service is not needed due to belief that our lifestyle would be intricately tied to the alleviation of the need of others
Thomas Hobbes	"Government best which governs most"	People, left to themselves are devoid of goodness	Individuals like Mother Teresa would be a far cry from Hobbes's concept of human nature	Community service mandated as means of control
James Harrington	Seventeenth-century philosopher	Man only acts in his own self-interest	Selfish nature of man. Love would be impossible—narcissism	What's in it for me?
Jean Jacques Rousseau	French philosopher	By ourselves we are good; when we mingle with others we become evil.	Steering clear of "bad company" criminals who admit that alone, they would not have erred	Difficult to find a motivating force for helping others when it places one in a contaminating position
Montesquieu	Wrote "Spirit of Laws," checks and balances philosophy	Individuals cannot be trusted with absolute power	Lack of trust	Least relevant in terms of community service

seems so simple, yet most people find it impossible to perpetually live by this premise.

After much deliberation, the Shawnee Mission Northwest CCC agreed upon six words for their mission statement. They waded through the writings of the five aforementioned philosophers and came to the

conclusion that, to a certain extent, much of what they all
would easily be summarized in the words "the doer of goo‹
good." All the students who elect to be members of the CCC
ious degrees of "goodness." One student put it this way: "W‹
ally incomplete and we complete ourselves by helping others.
other people for our own well-being. Goodness results from ı
right choices with regard to others.

There is no lack of studies that deal with community servi
look at two of them.

THE GLUECK STUDY

The husband and wife team of Sheldon and Eleanor Gluecl
pioneering studies on the nature of man as early as the 1930s.
looking at what attributes would predict delinquency in ch
adults. It would not be surprising if you were somewhat puz
how delinquency is related to community service, but there i:
a relationship. Most courts and social workers are relying
community service to correct social wrongs committed by yoι
and adults.

We know that "locking people up and throwing away the k
therapeutic value. It can actually harden the individual t·
greater life of crime. Johnson County, Kansas, averages a
thousand arrests of young people per year. Most of these fir
fenders are placed on some kind of community service progɪ
rect their antisocial behavior.

We are prescribing community service to correct, punish,
a young person who is already in trouble with the law. In ᠄
200,000 young people were tried as adults in our courts, t
number ever in American history. Many of these instances ‹
been avoided. The Gluecks identified four types of personaliti
domorph, ectomorph, mesomorph, and a combination of tl
can community service aid each of these personalities?

The endomorph is the "laid-back, easygoing" type of p
These people, when provoked, resolve their dilemma by siɪ
with someone else. "Let's go mess around," would be thei

expression. They tend to be slow-starters, putting off until later what they should do today. What the Gluecks discovered was that few people with this type of personality actually were found guilty of criminal behavior.

The ectomorph also fell into this category. Ectomorphs were the quiet, sensitive types. Almost regardless of the provocation, this type responds by wanting to be left alone. They would yell, "Leave me alone, get out of my face!" By being alone, they simply overcame any compulsion to antisocial behavior.

The mesomorph presented an entirely different scenario. This personality not only led in the criminal scene, but in all other problematic categories such as alcoholism and illegal drug usage. When provoked, this person wants to fight back. They strive to correct a perceived wrong. A cursory glance at in-house suspension will find a preponderance of this personality type. This type needs to funnel the obvious energy they possess in abundance. Community service can be a potential outlet and a creative solution to this excessive energy.

Through experience we find that many of the so-called incorrigible students in high school are some of the best students in a community service class. You can always count on them to come through when something difficult needs to be done. It is important to channel, not punish, students with this type of personality. They need their activities directed and, when possible, to be placed in leadership roles.

In 1965, the Gluecks gave a lengthy interview to *U.S. News and World Report*. They again stressed the importance of assisting the mesomorph. Love can be and should be "tough" for these types of young people. It was their opinion that if we fail to reach the mesomorph, it would result in a wave of criminal behavior unlike anything previously experienced. The past thirty-five years have certainly validated this prediction.

VICTORIA SECUNDA—*BY YOUTH POSSESSED*

The classic study *By Youth Possessed* by Victoria Secunda holds the same position. Secunda laments the fact that we actually study the wrong type of students. Her contention was that we are all too familiar

with the reasons why young people "go bad." Single parent:
esteem, bullying, and factors too numerous to mention are an
known delinquent indicators. She asks, "What are the factor
duce the proverbial 'good students'?"

Here again, the winning answer indicates that *the kids u
great deal of adult involvement in their lives turn out to be*
This is one of the reasons that a daily class of community serv
the student is exposed to many types of adult involvement, is
The service hours can be monitored and, if needed, tailorec
"type" of student.

A community service class was asked to describe the ad
meeting every day. Their response was almost unanimous.
that by meeting every day they created the routine of gooc
true, we learn what we live! Students often say that they just
cally do the good thing and that goodness has become a habi
of them.

The Rene Spitz study has had a great impact sociologicall
munity service. Human beings are social by nature and need i
with others in order to become well-developed persons. Stu
shown initial disbelief at how a study of this kind could have
conducted. This study can be used to help define a concept o
and why it is important that we actually do something to pro:

Spitz's study, found in Pitirim A. Sorokin's book, *The Basic
Our Times*, was conducted between 1940 and 1945, during Wo
Many children in France had been orphaned during the war. S
gether a small staff and instructed them to find as many of thes(
babies (the younger the better) as possible. They returned wit
babies. The staff gave each baby his or her own crib. When
hungry, they fed them. When they were cold, they covered t
tered the room temperature. When they were wet, they char
Under no circumstances were they to pick them up or even ta

Spitz brought in a movie crew and sporadically photograph
bies and the staff. In less than a month's time, it was evident
thing negative was happening with the infants. They were be
tremble and shake uncontrollably. Staff members found it
watch and not pick the babies up or speak to them. In fact, s(
staff members resigned under protest. By the conclusion (

year, twenty-seven of those babies had been found dead in their cribs. Seven more died shortly into the second year of the study. The remaining twenty-one died the third year.

On the death certificate of each, Rene Spitz wrote a very strange word next to Cause of Death: Marasmus. The word, which is Greek, means to wither and die for lack of affection. We could probably argue about the cause of the babies' deaths. Some would say that it was child neglect and exclaim that one should not treat babies that way! Others might say it was "failure to thrive" and that there was something wrong with the babies in the first place. Still others might say that it was all a matter of sensory deprivation. To be sure, any of us would agree that those babies suffered from attachment deficit and had no opportunity to bond with anyone. All fifty-five babies needed that certain something that we call "intimate human response" or love!

When asked why they use drugs, student responses represent a version of Marasmus. They said, "It doesn't matter, I just don't feel anyone cares about me!" "There has to be something more than just going to school or to a job." All of us are in need of approval, need to be and feel loved. We are not in need of anything profound, time-consuming, or expensive. Approval and love can take the form of a gesture, a kind word, a pat on the back, or a listening ear, but all of these can potentially have a life-and-death significance.

Miracles happen quickly after community service begins at a school. There is a community center a few blocks from a school and it has become one of the favorite places for courts to place students on diversion. In fact, many of the best students in these classes began their community service as a prerequisite of their status in court services. It is not uncommon for students to say that they are glad that they were assigned to the community center. They found it fulfilling to help people, and they desired to continue that service.

One of the most memorable examples of the effects of community service lasted more than two years. Rebecca Beyer, at the time of her initial enrollment in Northwest's community service class, was a junior and had well over a 4.0 GPA. Her family was closely knit and she felt that she wanted to "give back" something to the community. She chose a local nursing home for her service, where she befriended an eighty-five-year-old resident by the name of Emma.

This was a match made "in heaven." They visited every da:
even saw Emma on weekends and special occasions. Rebec
luctant to stay in the class on days that students were "in-ho
ning future activities. Rebecca's senior year, Emma had bec
of her family.

Rebecca was granted permission to introduce her friend to
school via an assembly. It was near the end of the school yes
becca would be leaving for Boston University in the fall. S
Emma's wheelchair to the front of the gym. In front of the
dent body, with Emma sitting at her side, she read the follow

It is easy to get caught up in being an active teenager. In the sw
vanced placement classes, school responsibilities, and soccer, tw
hours is gone before it truly has been appreciated. For the past t
there has been one hour of every school day that is completely st
and I have savored every moment.

Upon entering my junior year, I enrolled in our community se
ganization, of which I am now the president. During the class pe
have the opportunity to tutor young children, work with animals
ter, visit a retirement village or nursing home, or help out at a l
pantry. I tried each of these, but when I arrived at the nursing
knew I had found my niche.

At first, the activities staff at the center assigned me to Emma
she wanted someone to read the paper to her. Gradually, we be
ing up the paper later and later in the hour. Emma never even
the paper anymore. I have been visiting her for two years. I co
school day and on many of my days off. Sometimes we play car
times we read books, sometimes we visit, and sometimes we jus
side in the sun.

I know that my time there helps Emma. People tell me that all
What people do not know is this, Emma helps me just as much
am with Emma, the rest of the world fades away. Literary analysi
calculus tests, and memorization of amendments just do not see
portant. Emma helps me appreciate the simple things in life. Fo
every day, there is nothing more to life than vanilla wafers and m
eight-year-old friend and for that hour, it seems like all I need.

Without my Emma fix, the day is just not the same. I might g
without appreciating the clear blue sky. I might drive all the w
from school without noticing the fall colors. She is an amazing

When I go off to college, I will write her, like I do when I am on vacations, with extra big, thick letters so she can read the cards on her own. When I am far away, I will think of her shivering in the warmth of the sun, "Oooohhh, doesn't that feel good?" And it does!

Rebecca remains an active young college student. During her semester breaks, she visits the grave of her dear friend, expressing her love with a bouquet of flowers. Rebecca would be the first to reiterate that the "doer of good becomes good"!

The holidays afford the students many opportunities for expressive acts of kindness. For several years, the students have collected food for families in Kansas City, Kansas, at Thanksgiving time. Economic conditions in that city are some of the poorest in the state. The class enlisted the assistance of AmeriCorps to identify the families with the greatest need for food. AmeriCorps also provided a list of the contents needed for a typical food basket. They were stunned by the students' response to the food drive. AmeriCorps had to make three separate trips to the high school to pick up the items collected there.

Some teachers believe that community service is only for honors students. They are the only ones who can be trusted. Consider the case of Tara Thacker. She inspired everyone, even though she had a variety of physical challenges. Tara was completely dependent on others for transportation. She volunteered every day at an elementary school, assisting a kindergarten teacher.

Tara immersed herself in that class, celebrating students' birthdays, listening to their concerns, and purchasing gifts for all of them. One day, a little boy asked her if she would be his mother. What a compliment to Tara! She also went to all their evening meetings, plays, and special events.

Tara also adopted a "grandmother" at the Lakeview Retirement Village who was ninety years old. They became another match made in heaven! Before the school year was over, Tara had already logged in more than 100 visitation hours at Lakeview and she continued to visit her "grandmother" two hours a week during the summer months.

For her numerous efforts, Tara received a generous scholarship from the Lakeview Intergenerational Council and was also honored by the Youth Service Alliance of Kansas City. She also served as a member of

the Northwest High School CCC executive board. Comment
Rene Spitz study, Tara said that she had bonded with so man
als that they should live forever!

Community service classes include students with every le·
ity. Never turn any student away because of their physical or i
condition. Parents are grateful and in many cases join us in
projects. Victoria Secunda would have been proud of how th
people have bonded with adults and are at ease with any age

Each year, schools celebrate Black History Month in a varie
Frequently, schools hold an all-school assembly with a speci
Two years ago, Shawnee Mission Northwest tried somethin;
ferent. In addition to a speaker, Northwest invited a choir fror
elementary school in neighboring Kansas City, Kansas. The·
for a bus to bring them to school for a kind of "back-up" co
the speaker finished. The choir was composed of fourth-,
sixth-graders.

Excitement was high as the bus approached Johnson Co
their faces touching the bus windows, someone whisperec
where white people live." But as they came in sight of the h·
excitement turned into a giant inferiority complex. They be;
"Are we good enough to sing in there? What if they don't lil
matter how gracious the high school students were in welcon
they put their heads down. Many tried to hide behind thei
They hurried to the gym without so much as a look around.

The bleachers were filled with eager Northwest student:
mentary students could hardly be heard. At the complet
first number, the community service students instinctively
roared their approval. The choir's next number almost ble·
off! The children were suddenly inspired! When they i
leave, it was arranged for them to continue to sing during tl
periods. "Come eat with us," one Northwest student said.
extra food."

The service class had planned for this to only be a conce
somed into a human relations breakthrough. Many of the cl
pressed a desire to enroll at our school and one child wanted
we had a choir. All sixty children went to the choir room and s.
fect harmony with the high school a cappella choir. When it v

leave, their heads were held high. Again, and with no coaching, the community service students formed a gauntlet and gave each little singer a "high five." What an uncontrived example that the power of love works miracles!

For several years, this same service class has tutored students in the Associated Youth Services (AYS) program. The program contains students who, for whatever reason, have dropped out or have been expelled from a regular high school. They enter the AYS program to earn graduation credits. Every Thursday or Friday, several service students spend the entire day assisting students in the AYS program. Many of the AYS students could be referred to as "bad company." The community service students exhibit positive behavior and become role models.

One of the first projects was to give AYS two refrigerators and fill them with food. During the course of the school year, whatever food was left over from Northwest activities was given to the AYS students. Christmas and Thanksgiving were always special. Each AYS student received a Christmas bag filled with a sweatshirt, socks, basketball, football, electronic games, and candy. One AYS student, in tears, said that it was his first Christmas present ever!

Community service students are involved in the STARS (Students Taking Action to Reach Success) program. Many elementary students cannot be reached academically during the school day. Elementary teachers find it difficult to give much-needed individual instruction. STARS volunteers from the service class assist elementary students with their homework after school. It doesn't take long before real friendships develop and students begin to turn their academic and personal lives around. Some tutors clock in as many as eighty hours within a single school quarter. Many elementary students have begun to experience success for the first time.

Volunteerism is a response to a human nature that is characterized by freedom. Regardless of how you feel about the need or lack of it for community service in the school, having a daily class has additional benefits not yet mentioned. There is already a mechanism in place for the service class to meet any urgent need.

When the tragedy of September 11 occurred, there was a nationwide request for funds to aid the fallen firefighters' families. The principal at Northwest merely asked the service class to spearhead a building drive

for donations. Within two days, a check for $1,000 was on its v
York City as a token of the school's concern.

Community service is *not* optional and our human nature
plete without it. The effects of some things affirm their exist
is more than just making a living. Our lives are tied to the we
others. We have flippantly said on numerous occasions "it's ju
But there are some things that money cannot buy. We all nee
with someone and to become involved in the lives of others.
living lesson that students have the opportunity to learn thr
munity service.

It is apparent that self-centeredness is the scourge of our a
away at our very nature. Students are bombarded with media
to take care of their needs with no reference to the needs of
do our young people a tremendous disservice when we fail to
realize the necessity of including others in their life. The qua
interaction with others determines the quality of our own life
other people!

Whether we admit it or not, we all seek the approval of ot
cannot be learned; it is something we do. The majority of
good only because they have worked at it. Love is born and
ously dies at the hands of the lover. We need to create it ove
again or it will slip away. Community service is not an end in
way, a direction to go. Each day will convince you that the dc
becomes good.

CHAPTER SUMMARY

1. Five philosophers have attempted to contribute infor
   the components of human nature. We ask, what is the
   man nature of human beings and what is it we need fo
   human fulfillment?
2. The mission statement of the CCC adopts the convictic
   must perform good deeds in order to advance in goodr
   back from students confirms this basic premise.

3. The husband and wife team of Sheldon and Eleanor Glueck divided human beings into four personality types. Community service can be a potent means to absorb the excessive energy of one—the mesomorph.

4. Victoria Secunda cautioned both parents and teachers that "good" students are those who have a great deal of adult involvement in their lives.

5. The classic Rene Spitz study points out that human beings need to be involved with other human beings not only for personal growth, but also for their very survival. Without affection, the child will most certainly die.

6. Students can bond with the elderly at almost any age. Students exposed to the elderly for only an hour a day can experience a profound effect on their well-being.

7. Inner-city experience produces many of the same results as mentioned in the previous item. Marasmus affects us no matter what social conditions we live in. It has been our experience that the good students make the bad students better.

8. Minority groups of all ages are affected by simple charitable deeds and respond accordingly. Likewise, students who are getting their last chance also respond positively to the CCC program.

9. The secret for success is not found in better buildings or more attractive media or educational frills. It is the sincere involvement in the lives of others that has changed even the hardest of criminals.

10. Community service can and does affect human nature, and the transformation is swift and long lasting. Marasmus also has a definite negative effect on young people.

3

MECHANICS OF A COMMUNITY SERVICE PROGRAM

I don't know what your destiny will be, but one thing I do know: the only ones among you who will be really happy are those who have sought and found how to serve.

—Albert Schweitzer

A journey of any length begins with the proverbial first step. This is not just a willingness to give community service a try. The step entails a commitment to the realization that it must be an integral part of the student's curriculum. As Frank Scully said, "Why not go out on a limb? Isn't that where the fruit is?"

It is difficult to propose a new course for an established curriculum. Logically, we might assume that community service fits best as a social science offering. In one school, the school nurse directs the program! It is essential that the class "stand on its own." Community service is not an extracurricular adjunct to an already crowded schedule. Initially, the Northwest model scheduled the class during the final hour of the day. This made it possible for students to complete their service projects without missing core curriculum classes.

Linking the class to local city government is a strong recommendation. This partnership would guarantee students substantive service

projects. City representatives are eager to participate and wi
clude students within their governmental structure.

The secret of this class's success is the empowerment of stu
element of choice is a requisite. Gradually, an executive boa
with seven elected members. This was not a popularity con
member oversees a particular part of the program.

Aristotle observed: "dignity does not consist in possessing l
in deserving them." Society is quick to recognize and reward
ties of youth. Browse the numerous awards bestowed on the
Mission Northwest CCC. These are indicators of the class's
ness in the eyes of others. To paraphrase Woodrow Wilson: "\
seek these honors, but by the sheer genius of our people,
thrust upon us." Doing "good" provides reward. Performi
goodness, not awards, is the major objective.

CLASS DETAILS

The class is limited to juniors and seniors because of the ne
dents to provide their own transportation. There was a great d
cern about student drivers and passengers. In eleven years
members have not sustained a single car accident. Enrollmei
the signature of three individuals: the student, the parent oi
and the class sponsor. A copy of this contract can be found in t
section of this book.

Students at Northwest have an opportunity to enroll in c
service during six different hours. Multiple sections were cre
commodate all 480 students. Students can also enroll for four
and receive one-half credit per semester. A large number c
enroll for four semesters.

The service contract has a special clause. If the student is t
are immediately dropped from the course. They subsequentl·
credit, even if it is the final week of the semester. This regulat
to the nature of the work done by the students. The execu
unanimously votes this regulation into the constitution every
ancy is defined as checking out of school but not attending
sites. Students have proven to be so conscientious that few
dropped from the program. When trusted, they are trustwon

ORIENTATION

All's well that begins well! School days are few and must be used efficiently. By reviewing the philosophers and other studies found in chapter 2, students will produce a mission statement. This will provide a sense of commitment. Their statement will incorporate a "life-changing" component. The students will come to realize that they need one another. Service comprises a reciprocal role.

An effective opening exercise consists of students writing thank-you notes to a teacher or staff member of their choice. This "random act of kindness" remains anonymous. Recipients, often in tears, visit the class to express their gratitude. This activity was copied in a Russian school (chapter 6) with the same emotional effect. The act of service exemplifies the student's true orientation.

Students watch the movie *Lord of the Flies* (the original black and white version). What follows is a heated discussion. The shape of society depends on the ethical nature of an individual, not on any political system. Most students reach the conclusion that whatever defects are found in our social fabric can be traced directly to defects in human nature. The results of the circumstances quiz in chapter 2 are also debated at this point.

ON-SITE ASSIGNMENTS

Guest speakers invite students to visit their location. They provide much-needed information on the nature of the service required. Opportunities include the following: retirement homes, Alzheimer facilities, elementary and middle schools, community centers, and animal shelters.

Students are now ready for their initial experience in the community. A two-week trial period allows the students and the site to determine if they wish to continue the experience on an extended basis. Students buddy up so they can carpool to various locations. They pay for their own gasoline expense. Students check out individually with the sponsor. They sign in at their destinations. They are responsible for judging the length of time for transportation in order to return to their next class. If it is necessary to miss more than one hour of class, a Code Six form must be completed and submitted to the class facilitator. This ensures that the

attendance office, the parents, and the instructor are aw;
amount of class time employed.

TRUST

> This above all: To Thine Own Self Be True.
>
> —William Shakespeare

Trust is the key to a successful community service program. Ir
is an important part of the lives of each of us. A level of tru
sential to our lives that we do not appreciate it until it is gon(
that people who have processed and shipped our food have d(
scientiously. We trust the safety of our cars at seventy miles pe
a jet airplane at 800 miles per hour. But there is a tendency t
trust at the educational level.

A college professor had a unique way of demonstrating
grade in his class depended on a single exam, given at the enc
mester. The class was very intense. The instructor, after distri
exam, turned his back on the class. He began reading a b(
every opportunity, no one cheated!

We expect perfection from our adolescents. We never e
fection from fellow adults. The element of control in sch(
ond only to control in prisons. There is a need for proced
but one could question the extensive checking of permissio1
borders on active mistrust. Trust is a value that can only be :
doing. On day one, students in a community service clas
given complete trust. They lose it only if they abuse it. V
slowly becomes a habit, reliability results and a changed in
produced.

STUDENT CHOICES

Weekends and evenings can be spent doing chores at retirem(
helping at school carnivals, hosting various lunches and din1
nizing intergenerational dances, and so forth. Many students
selves volunteering well into fifty or sixty hours. The record

west is over one thousand hours in one school year! That student was also on the honor roll.

Retirement homes are gracious hosts to the service program. Activities may include adopt-a-grandparent program; a fishing derby; a picnic in which residents are paired with high school students; decorating for the holidays; Christmas presents to residents who have outlived their relatives and friends; talent shows; fashion shows; and many other spontaneous activities. One retirement village in Shawnee Mission responds with scholarships for students who average at least a hundred hours of service at their village.

The city of Shawnee utilizes students to clean long stretches of its highways and streams. The city has also requested student assistance to improve homes or yards of the elderly who cannot afford the improvements. Examples of some of these special projects are:

1. A dinner to raise money for the medical needs of a three-year-old boy. This netted a profit of $22,000. The students used the school cafeteria and kitchen and all the food was donated by local grocery stores.
2. Participation in a bone marrow match screening to find a match for a twelve-year-old boy and a senior boy who would die without it. Hundreds of students and adults from the community were type-matched and a match was found for the twelve-year-old. He is currently doing very well.
3. Garage sales are held twice a year. Each sale usually nets about $2,000. Whatever isn't sold is donated to the community.
4. Monthly generational dances are held at the school with about two hundred area senior citizens attending. The dances are held on a Saturday evening with dinner and dessert prepared and served by the students.
5. Faculty appreciation parties are usually held on a Friday after school and often special treats are placed in the teachers' lunchroom by the students.
6. A yearly pancake feast is sponsored by local Optimists club with the profits used for two CCC scholarships.
7. Tutoring for delinquent boys at Associated Youth Services occurs two days a week with students providing one-on-one attention. This is a relatively new project—I might add, highly effective.

8. Feeding poor families in a neighboring city for Thanks:
   ally involving up to four hundred families, with all 1
   purchased by CCC and delivered to the families. This i
   expenditure of over $4,000.
9. Helping at a thrift store where all the profits are used t
   mentally challenged.
10. Assisting with the Job Olympics at a junior college.
11. Providing a prom at Lakeview Village for the residents
    dents decorating, dressing up, and "dating" the elderl
    als attending. The students even provided a limousine i
    idents.
12. Painting a house of a man who had suffered a heart
    was unable to do it himself. They did it all in just u
    hours.
13. Holding book drives for an inner-city grade school.
14. Providing clothes, health items, food, and money for t
    of a recent tornado.

GRADES

How can one "grade" community service? Grades are set up
sis of time. A student can have only five excused absences
penalty. These absences include field trips and events sponsor
side classes. After five absences, the student must make up or
each hour missed. The grading system is based on table 3.1.
are figured by quarter. The most common grade is an A.

The CCC at Northwest is a semester offering. The total
hours is divided in half for the semester grade. If the student
hours the first quarter and forty hours the second quarter, it

Table 3.1.   Grading System

Grade	Hours Required
A	30 hours beyond class time
B	15 hours beyond class time
C	10 hours beyond class time
D	3 hours beyond class time
F	No hours beyond class time

in an A for the semester average. The executive board of the CCC felt that a student must do some volunteer work above class time in order to pass. All projects must be approved in advance.

THE EXECUTIVE BOARD

The executive board has genuine power. It possesses the power to overrule the class sponsor. The executive board decides which projects the class will undertake. The class must have a constitution, conceived by the executive board. Individuals become members of the board by submitting an essay to the current president and vice president, who in turn choose the students they feel will serve the CCC best. The class sponsor chooses the president. The president, in turn, chooses the vice president.

FINANCES

Funding is crucial to the successful operation of the community service class. Any money received by the class must *never* be spent on the class itself. Any funds that are raised must be used to assist those people who are in need. The class should not be a fund-raiser for the school.

Generally, monetary requests help individuals with utility bills, rent, and food. At the start of the semester, students are encouraged to bring twenty-five cans of food to class each grading period. Some programs put a cap on the amount of aid an individual can receive. The executive board reviews each request individually and decides on the amount of assistance.

Coupons for Education

Local grocery stores may agree to the coupons for education project. Students clip coupons from the newspaper. The retirement home residents can also cut out coupons. The coupons are attached directly to the products in the store. When customers choose that product, they are given the option of deducting the amount from their purchase or donating the amount of the coupon to the community service class.

The class will create professional signs that inform shopp
program. Students can even "sell" the idea to shoppers as the
store. The Northwest program raised $10,000 the first year o
The students feel a sense of ownership. As one student p
raised it so we could have a definite voice in where the mone

Garage Sales

Students place advertisements in the local papers and si
area to let people know about the garage sales. People fron
munity donate items for the sales. One family donated a car. (
of the sale, the students volunteer to arrange, sell, carry items
even deliver them for customers who cannot manage by the
is not uncommon for people to donate money rather than
items. "Keep the change" is a common refrain from custom
the sales. Many students and parents bring homemade food f
As someone once said, "One person's junk is another person's

Dues

Each student at Shawnee Mission Northwest donates at
month, or $18 a semester, to the class. Each hour decides w
money will go. Classes have bought children's books for an
school, provided food for the local community center, or s
money on school supplies for students who couldn't afford m
school. One class bought clothing for a student who only had c
of clothes. Dues are used as "petty cash" for the class.

Donations

As the reputation of the class increases, so will donation:
parents of reformed students donate large sums of money,
their student has left the program. The parents of the first p
Shawnee Mission Northwest donate $1,000 a year in gratituc
the program did for their daughter. Premium Standard Farn
a prize hog and even had it packaged so it could be sold. N
provides all the cups, drinks, and napkins, plus a monetary do

all the Northwest intergenerational dances. Once the community knows your program is legitimate, they will help!

Dinners

The Northwest class heard of a two-year-old boy who needed a life-saving operation. The operation was beyond the financial means of the family. The executive board had the mother bring the boy to school and they created a video. Fifteen copies were made available to the teachers at Northwest to show to their classes. The officers managed to have all the food donated for a taco dinner.

Dinner tickets were $5 each. Businesses donated goods and services for a silent raffle. The local news media covered the event. Afterward, at an all-school assembly, the boy's parents were presented a check for $24,000.

Teachers routinely give generous checks or have fund-raisers of their own for the class. School groups sponsor assemblies with an admission charge, which provides a generous donation for class endeavors. The class extends itself to the entire school, making everyone a participant in community service.

COMMUNITY CHRONICLE

A community service class may experience a loss of "class identity." Since the students go out every day, it is possible to lose a sense of co-hesiveness. The class published its own newsletter to address this concern. Each publication highlights some of the projects that members are doing. It can list future events, print letters of appreciation, and chronicle awards. Students are encouraged to write articles concerning their volunteer work site. A copy of the *Cougar Community Chronicle* is located in the forms section of this book.

STATE PRISONS

In association with a state prison system, students can learn that prisoners and parolees are individuals with the same kinds of problems as others.

Students realize that a parolee's history and incarceration make
for him or her to reenter society without some assistance. T
Correctional Institution is only twenty-six miles from Northwe
mates are invited to speak to the class. Students begin helping
convicts to acquire clothing, tools for a job, and so forth.
"hours" for their grades. There are individuals who can facilitat
tionship with your class at each institution. Proceed at a speed t
fortable, and provide much communication concerning this
your students' parents and the administration.

THE KANSAS LEGISLATURE

In the past few years, the Northwest class has drawn the at
the Kansas governor, Bill Graves. He gave the class the
highest award: The Spirit of Giving. During the 2002 sess
Kansas legislature, Representative Lisa Benlon introduced
would require every Kansas high school to offer community
its curriculum. Several students were asked to testify on be
bill. Northwest students created the following items for
discussion:

1. COST: It costs the school district *nothing*. No books, ι
   required. Students even provide their own transporta
   dents have raised well over $150,000 for various project
2. GRADES: Grades and student performances are enha
   of their other classes. Dr. Deborah Bogle did a 1994 dc
   sertation on the CCC and other local volunteer progran
   dressed the issue of grade improvement among those iι
3. SUCCESS: Students are almost guaranteed success. S
   all physical and mental abilities experience success ever
   one can mow, rake, plant, visit the sick and elderly, an
   any number of caring activities. Students are empowere
   own achievements and the praise of those whom they a:
   self-esteem also skyrockets.
4. PERFORMANCE: Students generally surpass basic ex
   and even under demanding standards of grading, the va

of students exceed the expectations for an A or B grade. No students have failed this class. Three were eliminated from the program for one truancy each.

5. COMMUNITY: Community evaluation of the school changes. Comments from the school board members attributed a successful bond proposal to the CCC. The local community becomes more involved with the school through donations to the program, asking for assistance, and positive comments about young people.

6. LEADERSHIP: Leadership qualities emerge very quickly and students take charge of their own learning and develop projects to help others. Self-motivation becomes the *norm*.

7. QUALITY: Quality students do enroll in this class and perform at the highest levels. Even students from the learning center, with limited academic ability, are able to participate in this program and do outstanding work and achieve high grades for the first time. Many of these students become leaders for the first time as well.

8. INTERGENERATIONAL: Intergenerational experiences are many and the bond that develops between the old and the young is nothing short of inspirational.

9. DIVERSION: Many students satisfy their diversion hours through this class. They not only perform their assigned number of court-mandated hours, but continue on long after they have completed their hours. One of the members of our executive board had been on diversion. One district court judge put a young lady in our program.

10. DISCIPLINE: Discipline problems simply do not exist. It is true that the "doer of good becomes good." Character emerges very quickly. Students in this class become sensitive to the needs of others.

11. DONATIONS: Students donate at times their entire paychecks for causes affecting the poor and needy. One student purchased fifty-five dictionaries for a group of delinquent boys and she had been in the program only four days. Students do contribute to the well-being of others.

12. YOUNG PEOPLE: The community's view and evaluation of young people changes in a positive manner. Gifts, cards of appreciation, participation in school events such as plays, sports,

and others increase. The media do more positive stc
young people.

13. PRIDE: Students take a greater pride in their schoc
ample, they have developed secret pals with their teac
vided faculty treats, sent cards to sick students, and
and special letters of appreciation to community pr
help with projects. The class has also developed an or
ter" in which each student writes their own feelings
sages.

14. SENIOR CITIZENS: Senior citizens are brought into
for lunches, class discussions, and other activities. Onc
special tables are set up for senior citizens to have lunc
dents in our cafeteria.

15. GRADUATES: Graduates of the school and the CC(
stay in touch by coming to school-sponsored events or
a volunteer program at their colleges. We have begun a
program to track the influence of the class on students
uate from our school.

16. TUTORING: A tutoring program has begun in the di:
posed of senior citizens from a retirement center ser
CCC. They also want to give something to the commu

17. IDENTITY: By linking the CCC program to the ci
ment, students have developed a genuine sense of c
and community identity. They attend city governmen
and the major city officials come to the school.

In March 2002, Gina Capps, an executive board member
west High School, gave the following speech to the Kansas le૬
support of a community service bill. This bill was based
Cougars Community Commitment classes:

When I imagine my future, I do not think of trigonometry, or cl
or of Shakespearean sonnets. I think of what I will always re
from my days at Shawnee Mission Northwest High School. Th
edge, I did not gain in a computer lab or after-school practice
or really even a classroom. I stand before you today and can
say that I had a chance to truly learn about people, and the re

outside of Johnson County through Cougars Community Commitment classes.

Too often in the daily lives of teenagers, one gets bogged down with monotony and day-to-day stress. The Cougars Community Commitment program allows students not only the chance to give back to the community, but to develop as a whole person and build character. My personal commitment to the CCC is what I am the most proud of.

I have worked extremely hard pushing myself academically for the past four years to maintain a 4.0 GPA. This pales in comparison to all the children that I've helped to learn their spelling words of the week and the huge smiles and hugs I've received after they earn their first 100 percent paper. CCC has opened my heart and my mind, and it has done much the same for hundreds of students before me. This class is a necessity. As our motto states: "The Doer of Good Becomes Good"!

House Bill 2352 passed overwhelmingly and went into effect July 1, 2002.

CHAPTER SUMMARY

1. The CCC program began as a separate independent class in the fall of 1992. It began small, with only seventeen students.
2. The class is limited to juniors and seniors because the students need to provide their own transportation. Students also need a genuine caring attitude about people.
3. The CCC was placed in the Social Science Department only because the sponsor was a member of that department.
4. The class meets every day for one hour. Currently there are ten sections of CCC.
5. The class has a president and vice president and together they choose an executive board, which approves expenditures and decides on special events.
6. The class uses various fund-raising techniques and activities, which include a schoolwide Dollar Day, garage sales, special dinners, and donations from the community.
7. Students sign a contract together with their parents and the CCC sponsor. A sample is included in the forms section of this book.

8. Letter grades are based exclusively on the number of h
   student serves in a project.
9. A Code Six form gives the student permission to drive
   cars and also to be gone from the school for the amou
   necessary to complete a project. A sample of this fo
   found in the forms section.

4

THE EFFECTS OF COMMUNITY
SERVICE ON STUDENTS

Practicing the Golden Rule is not a Sacrifice; it is an investment.

—author unknown

Parents have been sending their children to schools of great varieties over the years. Quarterly report cards track the student's progress in math, English, social studies, and other courses. There may or may not be a citizenship grade that informs the parents of their child's conduct. Now we have added an assessment in community service.

As in an academic subject, one expects the students to absorb the subject matter with a letter grade indicating the student's progress. So it is with community service. You can expect a change to take place in the student's life. The following are examples that document the substantive changes in the lives of students involved in community service at Shawnee Mission Northwest.

Heather D. was in Northwest's first community service class. School enrollments had already been processed. The class was to pick up the students who had enrolled late. Only four students attended last hour and Heather D. was, unfortunately, one of them.

Her reputation preceded her. She had been a "problem child" since her parents' divorce when she was in the sixth grade. There was nothing

about this senior girl that held any promise for success. This
periment in community service!

There wasn't going to be a class because there were so fe\
Disappointed, defeated, and quite pathetically the teacher ad\
four students, "There are not enough students to merit a com\
vice class, so I would suggest that you all see your counsel\
something else before the late enrollment closes." Heather st
up in her chair and rubbed her nose as if hit with a foul odor
until Thursday to see if I can get some more students," she st\
ically. She was probably adding insult to injury. What kind \
would follow *her*? Would she recruit drug addicts, attendance
and unmotivated students for whom the work would be a bur

On Thursday the teacher walked into a class of seventee\
Heather said with a sense of triumph, "Are these enough t\
class?" Her eyes locked on the teacher's for what seemed lil
nity. She was searching the depths of his soul. Heather exhibi
desire for acceptance and approval.

The teacher suddenly felt a kindred spirit and a "second ch
silence was deafening. He had bet against the class on that first
had never been a class like this before. They would meet each
disperse somewhere in the community. What about accountal\

Over a thirty-year career the teacher had always regarded
a student advocate. He suddenly remembered a class from 1
youth, they helped him develop a basic attitude of benevoler\
students. That positive student outlook was about to be test\
really trust students? Did he dare allow them an autonomous
community? Do people really have the capacity to change?

Sitting in front of him were seventeen young people recr\
acknowledged "problem" student. What did she promise the
an opportunity to begin a whole new approach to educatic
These were decisions of monumental importance and they ne
made almost instantly. Smiling, the instructor took a leap o
said, "Welcome! This will be the class of your life!"

They needed something to do and places to go. The teac
the mercy of Heather, the class leader. Together, with a frie\
lasts to this day, this young lady and the sixteen other student
eran teacher into the best education class he had ever had. H

gan spouting, "We need committees!" "There is a community center at 67th and Nieman." "Beth's father is a doctor." They were off and running! That evening, the sponsor recalled a Bible verse: "Strength is made perfect in infirmity." The best was yet to come!

Heather D. deserves more description of her impact on the class. She had already dropped out of school and returned at the insistence of her stepfather. Her grades from previous classes were average at best. Heather was tall, pretty, and had a great deal of potential. It was her reputation as a drug addict that threw up red flags.

She was known to sneak out of her house at night and rendezvous with fellow "druggies" in order to escape into a fantasy world. Her mother would set her bedside alarm every two hours. When she didn't find Heather in her bed, Mom would frantically begin a search to retrieve her from certain disaster. Who opens their door to such a young lady? She appeared genuinely interested in the well-being of others and insisted on putting an advertisement in the local paper listing free community services.

Suddenly, like the proverbial "big bite" for a fisherman, a family requested assistance. It was Heather who responded. She soon discovered that her worst day was someone else's best day. Heather began to give things away from her own home. "I almost had to tie the refrigerator down. Heather wanted to give it away. But how could I say no, I was getting my daughter back," her mother said. "I had been praying for this very moment."

Heather's grades started to rise. Her attendance was almost perfect. Most important, her drug use ceased. To the amazement of everyone, here was a young lady from an above-average home who would sit on dirty floors, fight off cockroaches, and spend hours with numerous less-fortunate families. People mattered to her more than anything else. There was no denying that it was Heather's class, and she led the other sixteen.

Heather found plumbers who donated their services. She collected money for utility bills after numerous calls. Heather single-handedly turned this class on. Simultaneously, she turned her own life around. She even had to choose between the prom or a crucial speaking engagement. It took her only seconds to choose the speaking engagement.

In the audience was Heather's mother. Her pride grew with each of her daughter's words. The class itself did not go unnoticed or unappreciated.

Soon came the award nominations from Prudential, Noxema, City *Star*, the Kiwanis, the Optimists, and Sertoma. J. C. Peni nated the class for its Golden Rule Award.

Flanked by the school principal, the class sponsor, anc mother, Heather listened as the awards were presented. Whe was chosen for the first prize, the sponsor said to Heather, " with the principal, it's your award." Heather arose and, shou back, acknowledged the standing ovation. Her mother was she witnessed the culmination of her daughter's transformati

Shortly after, with graduation only a month away, CCC stude up to speak at the evening ceremony. To the surprise of man was first on the list of speakers. On the evening of May 23, 199 rose to address a crowd in excess of ten thousand. Her five sheer eloquence mesmerized the packed house. Her meta complete, the doer of good had become good!

That night as the sponsor prepared for bed, he thanked C class that had changed Heather (and was to do so with man the subsequent years). Heather had learned a simple lesson do for others comes back more than a hundredfold. Now she life to the fullest. As Heather's mother and stepfather prepar that graduation night, a unique exhaustion and euphoria cam mother. Just before turning out the lights, Heather's stepfath that his wife was already asleep, but the alarm clock was not usual two-hour check. It would never be set that way again.

Heather D. is only one example of countless changes in st cause of their involvement in this first class. What appeared (face to be impossible soon became routine. The impossible came expected. To collect over $40,000 in a school year w ridiculous for a group of high school students. How these seve dents mastered this class and raised that amount was nothing miracle. These are the events of that story:

A letter from the local community center indicating that perfect project for the class was received with hesitation. $40,000 was needed to rescue a couple in the community. T laughed as he told the class that someone had requested $4 one else was laughing. Heather D. reminded the sponsor th dents made the decisions.

A local woman with spina bifida had had a life-saving operation at a local hospital. The bill was over $40,000. The couple had no insurance. It was early December and the hospital was suing the couple for the full amount. Because they could not come up with the $40,000, the couple was in danger of losing their home a couple of weeks before Christmas.

The class began their quest. In researching the case, they found that the couple had equity in their house. The students realized that the couple could probably borrow against the equity. The class sponsor was still skeptical! The students found a bank to handle the refinancing. Unfortunately, they would have to come up with $2,700 cash to cover refinancing fees.

One of the students suggested, "Let's have a Dollar Day here at Northwest and ask every student to bring at least a dollar." They made announcements on the school PA system. They hung up signs urging students to help. Groups of students went to classrooms with a personal appeal. They were under some tight time constraints because the bank had a firm deadline of Friday, one day away.

Dollar Day was held on Friday morning. By the time the last envelope was opened and the money counted, they had a grand total of $2,200, exactly $500 short of the goal. Unexpectedly, a community agency offered the CCC a donation of exactly $500. The principal grabbed the piles of money and made several trips to the bank. The bank volunteered to stay open until all the donations had been counted. The final amount was exactly $2,700. The woman's husband was relieved! Seventeen shining faces knew then that they could move mountains.

At the next Spirit Day, the wife requested time in the program to thank the student body for their generosity. Flanked by two CCC students, Alice was literally carried to the microphone. It was the tone of her voice and her obvious emotions that brought the students to complete silence. She began with a broken "Thank you." Someone in the audience shouted, "Hey, that's the lady whose house we saved!" The entire student body instantly rose and cheered. The students broke into a rhythmic chant, "Let's do it again! Let's do it again!" The associate principal came to the CCC sponsor in tears, hugged him, and sobbed, "Oh, this is so beautiful."

Since that day, Dollar Day has become a permanent fixture at Northwest. "Let's do it again" has been reiterated over and over. At the assembly,

the sponsor felt a rush of pride, humility, and elation. Heather
over to her teacher, put her arms around him, and cried. Much
a house was saved that day.

THE BURNING FURNACE

> We are like one-winged angels. It is only when we help each
> that we can fly.
>
> —author unl

Every day requests for assistance will cross your desk. You will
have tried everything else but without any luck." "We need $·
any agency can give us is $100. You are our last hope." "I find
to ask people who are much younger than I am for help, but
choice." One of the strangest requests came from a busines
from another school. The head custodian had come on hard
was in need of a furnace. Kansas's winters can be cold and thi
eight children. Furnaces are often expensive and difficult tc
this project would require professional assistance. True tc
agreement, the business manager never heard the word "nc
told the class would discuss what they could do.

David's furnace had gone out in late March and a new on
be needed until mid-fall. David had a second job. It was his ii
use the "extra" money to purchase and install a new furnace
had not counted on was a diagnosis of cancer, which made it
for him to hold down both jobs. He needed several operation
matters worse, David found it difficult, if not impossible, to
sistance from young people.

Although far from wealthy, David had always been self-suf
figured that other people needed help more than he did and h
vinced he would "make it." He could not leave much to chan
family. He finally accepted that it was just not possible for thei
be stretched to include a new furnace.

The budget manager's dilemma was compounded by Davi
of not accepting help. The class would need to keep their l
dential. This was the easy part, for the CCC never asked for r

of any kind. The class contacted the local community center. They were able to buy a new furnace at a wholesale price, but couldn't come up with an installer.

The students started calling a variety of furnace installers with no luck. They all wanted them to purchase the furnace and installation. The cost of this arrangement was prohibitive. Finally, a student found someone who would install the furnace for $200.

All was in readiness and the business manager approached David for the installation date. When he arrived at David's home, he heard him loudly speaking, "God, I didn't want cancer. All my life I have always paid my own way. I have provided for my family and there is nothing more I can do. I've done all I can do to heat my home for my family. You have to help me, please!"

The business manager knocked on the door and said, "David, a group of high school students wants to give you a new 150,000 BTU furnace and we can arrange to have it installed tomorrow if that would be all right with you." David just sat there on the sofa. Suddenly, with tears in his eyes, he slid to the floor on his knees, buried his head in his hands, and sobbed. His prayer had been answered immediately. The furnace was installed the next day. This was good timing, for the winter ahead was the worst Kansas had had in years.

When the installer was about to leave, David asked how much he owed him. The installer didn't hesitate to say, "It's all been taken care of by some high school group!" Once again, David sobbed tears of appreciation and relief. The furnace, in reality, was not a lot of money for a group of high school students. To David, it was a priceless gift that demonstrated God's love. Their motto was once again proven: "The doer of good becomes good." The students would do this for another family before the winter was over.

CHARACTER

The ultimate measure of a person is not where one stands in moments of comfort and convenience, but where one stands in times of challenge and controversy.

—Martin Luther King

Many of us have experienced tragedies at some time in our li⟩ fully, these setbacks have helped us develop coping mecha employ these when confronted with monumental life-chan⟨ cles. Sociologists call this the "continuity of socialization." ⟨ has been referred to as "inner reserves" or simply "an inner Unfortunately, tragedies that occur early in life are different challenging. In youth, our inner strength has not mature tested.

Heather F. was enrolled in sociology I and was a solid C st⟩ no special attributes. She needed an elective for graduatio community service class filled that requirement. Tragedy ⟩ Heather soon after enrolling. Unfortunately, she was too yoι sess the needed "inner strengths."

Heather F. woke up in the early morning and had a strong f something was wrong with her boyfriend. She quickly dι dashed over to his house. She found her boyfriend in the mid cide attempt. He was hanging from a tree in the backyarc grabbed his legs while screaming for help. When someone rived, John literally died in Heather's arms. He spoke no final left no note of explanation. A huge void surfaced in Heather'

After an extended absence from school, she returned anι her sociology class. You can picture the red eyes and the fre tant stares that dictated so clearly where her thoughts were. O simply turned to the wall and began to cry and scream! How one help save this junior girl from a life of grief and depres⟨ could the tragedy of her life be converted into a "happier" m

As so often happens, an elderly woman called who needeι to look after her two dogs while she was visiting her husband pital. Her husband, Don, had developed a severe case of e from using a blowtorch. The sponsor suggested to Heather F she and her best friend, Jennifer, join the CCC class and loo two dogs. Both girls eagerly embraced this suggestion.

Gladys was informed that these two young girls would comε to change the water, put out food, and walk the dogs. Thε Gladys bonded quickly. One day, Heather came to the screaming, "I've got to see Gladys right away!" There was no ⟨ hesitation. The sponsor urged her to go.

Both girls also went to the hospital and ultimately became good friends with Don. They even tried sneaking his two dogs into the hospital, only to be strongly reprimanded by the staff. Not to be outdone, they took pictures of Don's dogs and every now and then took them to the hospital. They were now "family" in every sense of the word. The girls cleaned, cooked, and ran all sorts of errands for Gladys and Don. The best was yet to come.

Don was scheduled to return home in two weeks. Gladys was concerned about the peeling ceiling in his room. Plaster dust was falling, which was dangerous for Don to breathe. It seemed that a new ceiling was the only solution. Heather and Jennifer enlisted the assistance of the school "druggie," Matt. Matt was also in their sociology class, but frankly he was "high" so frequently that passing was out of the question. The girls measured and ordered drywall. They purchased nails and tape. Matt thought the ceiling fan should be replaced so the girls bought a new one.

They waited with the class sponsor for a Saturday delivery of materials. Heather and Jennifer read a book from the library on how to install drywall. The deliveryman, after learning what they were doing, tore up the bill. He stayed that entire morning to help put up the ceiling. Matt volunteered to put in the new fan when an electrician could not come for more than a week.

It seemed all was going too well. The ceiling was up, the seams were taped, and the girls were proud of what they had accomplished. The finishing touches were up to Matt. He proceeded to turn the fuse box off (a good beginning) then separated the wires. It was obvious that he had a "chemical" boost. The sponsor handed him tools, tape, screws, a hammer, and other items that he needed. Finally, Matt said he was finished and the fuse box was turned back on.

Matt turned on the switch. Nothing happened! He didn't understand why. The sponsor was more than disappointed and angry for letting him do it in the first place. Suddenly, he realized that there was a chain switch that needed to be pulled to start the fan and he pulled it. The blades started and spun faster and faster. The look on Matt's face was one of complete surprise, elation, and accomplishment!

Later the girls returned with wet rags to work on the seams. The house was finally ready for Don's return. Several days later, Don came

home. Gladys had not told the girls that he was coming ho
One week later, Don was gone.

The local funeral director called the CCC sponsor at hom
that Don had requested class members to be his pallbearers. (
call to Heather is all it took to arrange for eight CCC girls t
carry Don to his final resting place. Shortly after the funeral,
to see the CCC sponsor. He had cut his hair and it was obvic
wasn't using drugs. "Mr. Poplau," he said, "I know that I can'
sociology class, but I don't need it for graduation. Can I stay
way? I need the time to work on my other classes in order to
There was no hesitation on the teacher's part. After the othe
left that day, the teacher turned out the lights and cried tears

All three of these students are doing well and often return
to visit their former teacher. In addition, Heather's brother al:
CCC class and did outstanding work. When Heather and J(
turned last year, they were asked what got them through th
tragedy. Heather said, "Well, at first it was the dogs and then
much Gladys loved Don. We agreed that if we could he
through her crisis, that we could get through ours." The "doe
becomes good one more time!

THE GANG SHOOTING

> The highest exercise of charity is charity towards the uncharit
>
> —author unl

CCC students are always alert to human catastrophes that br
to persons or families. Even though the person may or may n(
ties to the school, it makes no difference to those enrolled in c
service. One such case involved a young married man who be(
tim of a drive-by shooting. This "good Samaritan" was approa
ride at the end of a party. As generous as Mike was, there wa
question that he wouldn't help. As he left with his passenger
he know that he was being followed.

At the time, Mike had two children, a girl aged two-and-a
nine-month-old baby boy. He had also been taking care of

mother. As his passengers left his car, another car pulled up and opened fire. Mike took five shots to his head and five to his torso. He survived, but with disastrous physical damage. Most of his tongue was blown away. His lower jaw and nose were gone. He lost his cheekbones. He would never be able to smell or taste anything again.

Needless to say, CCC students wanted to help. Because Mike was permanently disabled, he needed a computer to work at home. The class bought him some clothes, a computer, and miscellaneous items for Christmas. They never met Mike but they have a good feeling that they helped this young man. Mike knows that there is a group of young people out there that he can count on for further assistance. Slowly his doctors are rebuilding his face, and the CCC is helping to rebuild his life and self-esteem.

HENRY

Charity sees the need, not the cause.

—German proverb

For eleven years, I volunteered at the Kansas State Prison in Lansing, Kansas. There I met with convicts of every description and crime. In fact, I met several of my former students serving time at this institution. I soon discovered that the unique problem that faced the inmates was their return to society. Many either didn't have employment waiting for them, or they had been incarcerated for so long that life on the outside was unfamiliar to them.

Such a person was Henry Floyd Brown. He had spent a total of fifty-four years in various prisons in his lifetime. He was an intelligent man and had earned a B.A. degree while at Lansing. When he was granted parole, a multitude of adjustment problems faced him.

Upon his release from a halfway house, Henry found an apartment devoid of any furniture. He didn't have any money. The CCC met in executive session and felt that they could obtain sufficient furniture to make his apartment livable. Henry took possession of his apartment. At the same time, CCC students gave him a truckload of furniture. They even bought him food and later gave him clothing.

In gratitude, Henry put a picture of the group on his cor
reminder of his promise to "go straight." Now, five years late
doing well, has authored a book, unionized his shop, and onc
named employee of the month! This simple act of kindness b
currently saved the Kansas taxpayers nearly $200,000.

The class was so pleased with this venture that they l
touched the lives of other ex-offenders. Racks of clothes of va
sit in the back of the classroom for ex-convicts to take free
The classroom itself became a place for ex-convicts to meet
adjust to life outside prison. This activity cost little, but had
effects for the men and for society. In effect, the school has
kind of "halfway" house for both men and women. A call to
role officer will connect ex-offenders with the CCC. The ben
sides is immeasurable.

THE $500 MIRACLE

Small deeds beat great intentions.

—author unl

A young man from a sister high school in the district trar
Northwest and was placed in the CCC sponsor's sociology
done with all new students, he was asked to introduce him
class and tell why he chose to attend Northwest. The class w
at his openness. He spoke of how his family had disowne
though they lived in the area, they wanted nothing to do with
sequently, he was living alone and had an evening job that
teacher's salary. Within a short time Larry had his head on th
never turned in any assignments and often put his head dow
The teacher visited with him privately only to find out th
worked all night and had no time to do homework. He defi
"Look, Mr. Poplau, I am making more money than almost an
school. I don't need your class to be successful!"

About two months later, Larry told the sponsor he had lost
chef. He needed food and a place to live. He confessed that h
living on the street and selling his body for money. The degra

all had changed him and had taken all of his self-esteem. He had become a real cipher. He eventually went to California with his girlfriend, where no steady work materialized for him. He was utterly, totally dependent upon his girlfriend for support. He had no family, no friends, no transportation, no job, no high school diploma, and no positive outlook for the future.

Ultimately he stalked a woman at an ATM machine and robbed her at knifepoint. He was arrested and sentenced to two-and-a-half years in jail. Since he was wanted in Utah for a similar crime, he was transferred to a prison outside of Salt Lake City. After a year in prison, his parole officer called to see if Larry could return to Kansas when he was paroled. Larry needed transportation, money, a good job, and a place to stay. The CCC agreed to help him.

The class found him a job in a pet store. The owner offered him a modest room in the basement amid all of the boxes of supplies. Larry never hesitated and moved into the small quarters. The class gave the local community center $500 to distribute to Larry in small amounts. Part of the money went immediately for clothes and food. The community center supervised Larry's first month, only giving him money on proof of need.

On the last day of school that year, Larry, dressed in a suit and tie, walked into the CCC classroom to thank the students for their faith in him. He was the salesman of the month at a cleaning company and is about to get married. He wanted to personally thank the class for their investment. The teacher could not remember a harder hug or a more sincere thank-you than the one from Larry as he left the class and went out of their lives. This was simply another example where "the doer of good becomes good."

THE SENIOR PROM

When we hear the word "prom" we normally think about high school juniors and seniors dressed in formals and tuxedos, with proud parents recognizing that their child has matured into young adulthood. Who would think that a senior boy's date would be a ninety-one-year-old woman?

CCC students planned and executed their supreme achievement with a Senior's Prom titled "A Time to Remember." The event was held at

Lakeview Retirement Village. Men and women in their ei
nineties danced cheek to cheek with people seventy years tl
They had pictures taken together and shared a limousine rid

About thirty students spent the better part of a Saturday
the lounge at the retirement home. The students paid for all
lowing favors themselves: flowers, streamers, decorated tables
grape juice dispensed from an ornate punch bowl, and a li
piece band.

At 7:00 P.M. the lights dimmed. With a feeling of mutual r
love, the intergenerational evening began with a spirit unmai
by their own high school prom. The evening climaxed with 1
ing of the king and queen, drawn at random, beneath a balloo
added an air of authenticity.

One "young-at-heart" senior citizen sought out the spor
conclusion of the evening's festivities. He said that the ni
dream come true for him. He had missed his own high sc
decades ago. In jest the teacher said to him, "Don't tell me tl
some man like yourself couldn't get a prom date!" In tears an
vious emotion he said, "Mr. Poplau, it was World War II and
drafted—I missed my prom."

"A Time to Remember" had a variety of memories for each
attendance. One senior lady confessed that this was the first ti
danced with a man since her husband died. Returning home tl
after the "prom" was like hearing "Joy to the World" for the fi

WHERE ARE THEY NOW

It is in the shelter of each other that the people live.

—Irish p

Ten years later, Heather D. is now a college graduate. She is ha
ried and holds a responsible job. Both she and her mother freq
Northwest to express gratitude for what her mother calls "a
God!" Almost every Christmas, Heather's mother and stepfat
$1,000 to the CCC. They have said, "This is what we would hav
Christmas. Our Christmas is having our daughter back with us!

Heather F. and Jennifer are also college graduates. Each one comes in once in a while to visit and express gratitude for what the class has done for them. Gladys has moved to another city. Before she moved, the CCC had a birthday/going-away party for her. Nearly everyone cried tears of gratitude. She and Heather F. continue to correspond and share their lives with each other.

Alice and her husband still live in their home that was saved by the CCC. In gratitude they come to all the school's play productions, choir, and band concerts. Frequently they attend monthly dances held by the CCC. Without fail, the class always remembers them during the holidays.

Henry is now off of federal parole and will be taken off his state parole in six months. New CCC members visit him in his apartment and always bake something to brighten his day.

Former CCC students often return at spring break and share what they are continuing to do for others. One former student came home after just one week to get a washer and dryer for a needy family close to the college. Another young man says that he has formed the Brothers Committed to the Community, or the BBC, at his college, and his entire dorm is involved in helping others.

Wedding invitations come once in a while. All these things enable past students to say, in their own way, how the class changed their lives for the better. Nearly all cards and letters repeat our mission statement, "The doer of good becomes good."

CHAPTER SUMMARY

1. A new outcome of education must be to change the lives of our young people. All too often activities in today's society affect our young people adversely, such as drugs, crime, and lack of self-esteem. Schools must give all of our students an opportunity to develop goodness.
2. Students from adverse home situations, such as divorce and abuse, can receive the necessary opportunities in a community service program, to develop coping skills as Heather D did.
3. Tragedies can occur at any age, with most adults having already developed an inner strength or "reserves" that enable them to cope

and grow from setbacks. And any student can develop tl
needed to cope with tragedies that they might experie
Heather and Jennifer learned to deal with suicide and
and are doing fine years after their graduation.

4. Young high school students can be a source of strength
    who find themselves dealing with almost insurmounta
    cles. A simple furnace can make a profound difference i
    being of a family.

5. Students learn that there is a solution to a $40,000 p
    coming up with the money to save a couple's home.

6. Ex-convicts have difficulty dealing with reintegration ii
    upon release from prison. Students learned the quality
    ness by helping an ex-convict who spent fifty-four years

7. A $500 donation and a show of caring from students ma
    ference in a young man's life.

I am always asked for statistics and if our program is making a
in the lives of young people. These stories represent the "st
this change.

5

AN INTERGENERATIONAL
SERVICE MODEL

A gift consists not in what is done or given, but in the intention of
the giver or doer.

—Seneca

Lakeview Retirement Village is located about ten minutes from Northwest High School. It is a dynamic complex filled with retired residents
of every description. It quickly became the location of choice by nearly
half the CCC students when selecting their work site. The volunteer director, Evelyn Ewing, is nothing short of being a true "angel of mercy."
She not only understands the needs of the elderly, but she also has a
winning way with young people.

At the start of each new school year, Evelyn visits the classroom for an
entire school day. She invites the students to come to Lakeview Village
for their community service. Evelyn insists on some basic rules. The students who volunteer for Lakeview have a period of probation. She says
to the students, "Try it and if it isn't your cup of tea, Mr. Poplau will find
something else for you to do."

In the ten years that CCC students have been involved with Lakeview,
they have adopted grandparents, performed in talent shows, played cards,
danced, taken long walks, planted flowers, enjoyed conversations,
mourned the deceased, and became mature and caring individuals.

Shortly after Christmas one year, a CCC student called nearly hysterical. She said that her ninety-two-year-old "gra had just died. Four months ago, they had been complete st was as if a "family" member had passed away.

Each resident is eager to pass on the wisdom of his or he CCC student began to interview Lakeview residents on video. cluded the residents' memories of World War II; the Depres their families were like; life in the 1930s; and their feeli Franklin Delano Roosevelt. These videos were shown to othe on closed-circuit television.

Residents began to share and embellish experiences. One e year-old woman said, "I guess I do have a lot of living left to tually, the residents began to come to Northwest and serve concerning marriage, preparing for death, and history revie Alex Haley who aptly said, "When an old person dies, it is tl an entire library burning down."

Because this place has become so special to our group of Evelyn Ewing was asked to put the Lakeview experience i The next few pages contain the ten-year summation of the Lal lage experience and the involvement of the CCC students as Evelyn.

THE LAKEVIEW VILLAGE STORY AND THE COUG, COMMUNITY COMMITMENT BY EVELYN EWING,

From the streets of San Francisco to the streets of a small munity in Pennsylvania, young people want someone to liste They want a person they can trust and share their hearts with who will not judge them for what they have done but who will encourage them. Young people all over America need an old sible adult to be their friend.

Older adults who have outlived many of their friends or d family living close to them can become very lonely. If they li tirement community, assisted living, or nursing home they r ate mainly with adults and only catch a glimpse of children come to visit with relatives in the facility.

In 1992, Lakeview Village hired a volunteer director to form a volunteer department made up of residents. In 1993, the director proposed to the administration, staff, and the community of residents an idea of allowing children to come into the village and volunteer. It took a year before the residents and staff agreed to try the intergenerational idea of children volunteering at the village.

The Cougars Community Commitment (CCC) began volunteering at Lakeview Village back in 1993, at a time when most young people were viewed, according to many media reports, as only being interested in drugs, sex, and rock and roll. The students from Shawnee Mission Northwest High School were rated by folks in our county as students from the most liberal school in the Shawnee Mission school district.

For instance, it was the first school to have a smoking area for students. A year later, the school revoked this privilege as the attorney general of the United States published the stats concerning cancer and smoking. This high school had a large number of students from wealthy families and these students, on the surface, appeared to have little, if any, regard for others. Note the statement "on the surface," as it later became very obvious "kids are kids." In the CCC, economic backgrounds have nothing to do with the success of this group.

Before becoming the volunteer director at the village, I had been working with the CCC students and their sponsor since 1991. The students were volunteering to help put grocery store discount coupons on products in the stores. At the time, the volunteer director worked at the Johnson County Area Agency on Aging and received funds from the participating grocery stores in the "coupon program," which assisted in funding programs for the elderly.

One year after moving to Lakeview Village to start a new volunteer program and department, I contacted the CCC and asked if they were interested in helping start an intergenerational volunteer program. Could the school allow students to volunteer at the village during school time? They said, "we'll see what I can do."

For the past nine years, the CCC students have formed ongoing relationships with the residents and staff of Lakeview Village. Many of the students continue to come back and visit during breaks from college and after they are married.

This relationship of the young and elderly could really benel
groups. The structure of this Intergenerational Volunteer Pr
strong guidelines for the students. The students' time at the vil
not just be time away from the regular classes, as a time to p
out of school for that hour. The CCC strong motto, "The Doc
Becomes Good" became the creed for all the students to follc

In the beginning, most of the students were communicatii
tle with adults. In these beginning years, the population of se
living in the Lakeview community totaled 300; the number c
coming to Lakeview averaged about fourteen, three days a w

In the beginning of the Intergenerational Volunteer Pro
CCC student was a tall young man with long hair and a be
cut-off jeans shorts and various T-shirts. The Berkenstoc
added to the impression of a typical drug-addicted teenager
of the students gave the same impression by their choice c
clothing. Some of the other students did not display this ty
dress style, but in the eyes of the residents they were irr
teenagers regardless.

The tall young man with a beard was scary to many of the
for they had seen on the TV news story after story about teei
their criminal escapades and, unfortunately, he looked like tl
had not been coming for more than two or three weeks whc
unteer director's phone began to ring off the wall with neg
ments about him from residents not even involved in the prc

The comments included, "Evelyn, what is the idea of just
kind of kid come in here to volunteer?" I responded, "What do
any kind of kid?" "Well, you know, the hippie look, pot-smoke
kid." I said to the resident, "Oh, you mean Ryan, the studei
long hair and beard?" "Yes, that's the one!" I said back, "Well, .
a pot-smoking kid. Have you talked to any of your neighbors
had Ryan come and help them with chores?" "Well, no, but. .
rupted, "Please talk to your neighbors and see what they say
help that they are getting from Ryan."

Within two weeks, a number of residents were calling on a
requesting that Evelyn send them "Jesus." When I receive
phone call with this request, I had to stop and think, "W
world? Is this a senile resident with dementia or what?" Then

idents went on to say, "You know, the kid that looks like Jesus that has been helping my neighbor."

Ryan became one of the most requested students that came to volunteer. He truly exhibited a Christ-like nature such as being very kind, gentle, and willing to do whatever needed to be done, even coming back after school or on weekends to finish a chore that he could not get completed during the hour he was at the village.

At the end of the school year and during a celebration and reflection time with the students and the residents, several residents came to me and said, "Thank you for bringing these wonderful students to Lakeview. You've really taught us a lesson; you cannot judge a book by its cover. These students are God sent to us as they really care and are really nice." The residents had a big attitude adjustment through their encounter with the initial CCC students, and began a long-term relationship with Shawnee Mission Northwest High School Cougars Community Commitment classes.

In 1997, a Lakeview resident, Dr. Jack, had lost his longtime traveling companion and friend to Lou Gehrig's disease. He had suffered two strokes followed by severe depression and remained in bed most of the time. He was also becoming weaker and his doctors predicted he would only live a few more months at the rate he was going. Dr. Jack was just plain giving up on life in general. The Health Center staff and his doctors knew that Dr. Jack could be up and walking around enjoying life, but his grief and depression became just like a comfortable blanket that he kept pulling up around himself.

During this period of time, many residents had been calling me to comment on one very positive, upbeat student named John. I asked John to just visit with Dr. Jack and see if he could be a friend to him. This was shortly after the beginning of the school year and John agreed to give it a try.

At the end of John's hour of volunteering, he came rushing into the volunteer office saying, "Hey, Evelyn, thanks for introducing me to Jack. He is just great and we really hit it off. He has traveled all over the world, and he is going to help me by telling me what I need to study in order to become a doctor. I'm going to come back after school today. Dr. Jack is so cool."

In just one month, John had convinced Dr. Jack that if he asked the physical therapist, he could get a walker and they could be walking

around the village. If Dr. Jack accomplished this, John woul(
ing Jack out to McDonald's on Saturday for lunch. Two m
went by and Dr. Jack was walking with just the aid of a cane f(

In March of that year, Dr. Jack and John made plans '
guardian to go scuba diving in Florida on spring break. At the
week, they both returned with good tans. They were lau
shared stories with the other residents about their adventures
water while scuba diving. They described, in great detail, tl
the beautiful coral that they had seen.

John had succeeded in bringing this elderly gentleman b;
world of darkness into which he had been slipping. They h;
good friends and the difference in age seemed of little import
ther of them. John was so excited when he realized that he co
remarkable difference in the life of another. Dr. Jack had a ne
ation for young people and realized that if the day came whe
enjoy being around a young person, he would really be old. Joh
even invited Jack over for dinner on several occasions and als
him at Thanksgiving. Dr. Jack was now considered part of the

That year, John was awarded the J. C. Penney Golden R
along with $500 for his CCC class. The award was for John's c
and encouragement with Dr. Jack, helping Jack to see that hi;
still be productive and that his influence could be far-reac
mentored and developed relationships with other students
When John graduated and went off to college, his younger br(
adopted Jack the next school year. Year after year, the relatio
Jack and other CCC students has continued.

In another situation, Andrea, a student from another cc
school district, paid out-of-district tuition to attend Northw
join the CCC. She chose to come to Lakeview Village becau
a close relationship with a grandmother who had Alzheime
and she missed the wonderful times that they had shared tog
drea wanted to join the "Adopt-a-Grandparent" program at
and adopt a lady to be her surrogate grandmother. I match
with a ninety-four-year-old woman who had never married a
one to visit her—she was totally alone and lonely.

They immediately hit it off and the relationship flourishec
dream was to become a dress designer and Charlotte, he

grandmother, had had a former career as a professional dress designer. One time, Charlotte taught Andrea how to take an ordinary newspaper and make a dress pattern. The two-year relationship benefited both Charlotte and Andrea greatly, in spite of the difference in their ages. Ultimately, Charlotte influenced Andrea to go to Chicago where Charlotte had worked professionally and taught dress designing. Today, Charlotte is 100 years old and they still keep in touch. When Andrea comes home from Chicago, she always visits her dear friend and adopted grandmother Charlotte.

In 2001, the Lakeview Village Intergenerational Advisory Board awarded one $1,000 scholarship to an outstanding CCC student volunteer. In order to be chosen for this award, the student had to have volunteered at Lakeview and completed an application process. Since then, the residents had been making contributions to the scholarship fund all year and two scholarships were awarded in May 2002.

For the past ten years, we have watched students' lives being changed by the confidence they have gained as they interact and build relationships with the elderly residents of Lakeview Village. Students, who had no direction or plans for college or the future, have been making important plans in choosing a career field and a college, and continue to do so as they are influenced and mentored by their elderly friends at Lakeview.

The students enhance the lives of the elderly residents at Lakeview Village in so many ways. The residents, in turn, give the students an ear that will listen to anything the student wants to share, a nonjudgmental attitude, unconditional love, and friendships that last for years as residents and students stay in contact even after their volunteer service is completed. The residents tell students that "you can achieve your dreams if you work hard" and the students believe them!

At Lakeview Village, CCC students are called "our kids." Residents who interact with students daily will not tolerate anyone saying anything negative about the youth of today. The residents say, "If every school in America had a CCC class, maybe guns would not be brought into schools and students would not be shooting other students and teachers."

It takes the vision, passion, and commitment of a dedicated teacher and volunteer director to make the CCC programs and the Intergenerational Volunteer Programs and Service Learning projects work at

Lakeview Village. The CCC and Intergenerational Voluntee1
and Service Learning Project can be successfully duplica
America and around the world. Programs and schools can b
in changing and influencing students, one at a time, in order
plish acts of kindness through our example.

Together, we have ten years of success stories to share th
strate that lives have changed dramatically and that stuc
gained personal confidence when mentored by elderly resi<
conditional love, respecting, and valuing the accomplishmen
tential between both generations makes the partnership bet\
and Lakeview Village an overwhelming success. The wisdom
the elderly combined with the energy and the thrill of adven
youth bring these generations together in ongoing and gro
tionships.

Lakeview is the place where generations can form allian
reaching influences. It is beyond doubt that generations of y
ple and senior adults will continue to be a vital part of the Lal
lage community in the years ahead, and that the CCC p
Shawnee Mission Northwest High School will continue to
mold the students who are our future.

CHAPTER SUMMARY

1. The CCC classes have developed a successful working r<
   between Shawnee Mission Northwest High School and
   Village Retirement Center because of the dedication c
   class sponsor and volunteer director at the village.
2. The relationship between the CCC and Lakeview Villag<
   tory of over ten years and a multitude of services perfor1
   students and monitored by the residents.
3. Young people and the elderly alike need caring, givin
   ships in their lives and Lakeview Village has provided b<
   and the elderly for one of the CCC students' most p<
   successful volunteer experiences over the years.
4. The CCC and the Lakeview Intergenerational Voluntee1
   and the Service Learning Project teamed up to provide 1

life-affirming relationships for both students and village residents. The Intergenerational Volunteer Advisory Board works closely with the CCC to offer appropriate and rewarding experiences for the students who volunteer and also have developed a scholarship for deserving students who volunteer at Lakeview.

5. Various stories of the dramatic changes wrought in both the CCC students and the village residents validate the worth of the intergenerational project at Lakeview and the appropriateness of duplicating this program across America.

6

FROM RUSSIA WITH LOVE

Keep on sowing your seed, for you never know which will grow—
perhaps it all will.

—paraphrase of Ecclesiastes 11:6

In 1941, World War II and the Stalinist era were in full swing. The Cold
War was in full swing. You always knew when church services here in the
United States were concluding because the final prayer was for the con-
version of Russia. In addition to these timely events, my father was a
German immigrant who had the mindset that Germany should have
been allowed to vanquish the Soviet Union before its final defeat.

One of my most vivid memories of this period was a long walk with a
church pastor. There was a feeling in the world that America was doomed
because the Russian military would soon completely destroy us. He con-
firmed that many people felt the same way.

As the years went by, many people put their lives on the line fighting
the "Communist menace." Who could forget the words of Nikita
Krushchev, "We will bury you!" The largest nation appeared to be the
strongest nation.

Right-wing conservatives believed that the evil empire would somehow just go away. It would seem ludicrous to one day visit a country that
was determined to wipe out American freedom.

The outstanding volunteer work of the CCC had caught numerous education officials in this country. The students we sible for the numerous accolades that their instructor has rec tional Teachers Hall of Fame, Mid-America Teachers Hall of so forth. Without the students' generous, caring service, the C have remained only a dream.

As a result of these prestigious honors, the American Co former American Information Service), funded by the U.S. gc invited the CCC instructor, as well as other progressive educa the United States, to travel to one of the newly independent st as an educational adviser.

There was a preliminary meeting at the University of Del; a large delegation of teachers from the former Soviet Union. ticipant had to list in order the countries they wished to visit. no guarantee they would receive their choice. The message o would be taken to Russia.

It was suggested that gifts be brought for the people. The dents had, independent of their teacher, shipped two giant bo to Russia prior to the trip. The Russian teachers filled bag afte pencils, cards, pins, books, erasers, notebooks, travel guide; and cups. They seemed to be envious that all these items w(them personally, but for their students. Teachers, the world ov most altruistic people.

Each of the teachers selected for this trip represented a spe program. A few programs were selected to give a presentation; sians. The CCC was chosen as one presentation. There was so i gage" from the Cold War era to overcome. Russians, who had l bers of the Communist Party, would be the hosts. Richard W said, "How can I act naturally when I am thinking about acting

The Russians we encountered were very intelligent, well and spoke perfect English. Unfortunately, outside of a few p; one of the visiting Americans spoke Russian. The presentation stacked with CCC handouts for everyone to take. Although prehensive and nerves, the thought of CCC students provi(and motivation beyond measure. They had been responsible f ing the honor to take their program elsewhere. I said a praye live up to the Northwest students' expectations!

The Russian educators had notebooks and pencils ready to take notes. There are times in every person's life that one is truly inspired, and such was my case that afternoon. They listened with rapt attention and deluged the sponsor with questions. They loved it! Many wiped away tears or spoke in emotional English. These teachers from the former Cold War might accept a program literally designed to make the doer of good become good!

That group of Russian teachers was the finest audience ever. The sponsor was never alone while in Russia. Their interest was genuine and their comments inferred that they would replicate the CCC program in their schools.

There was great competition among the Russians for the group to visit certain cities. One teacher in Siberia went out of her way to describe all one could expect in her city. There were art galleries and a symphony. She even promised that every effort would be made to keep the sponsor warm! Another teacher promised orange juice *every day*. She made a special point to explain what a hardship that would be. She then added, "then after you leave, we won't have it anymore!" The sponsor began to feel like a rock star!

My chief satisfaction however, was that the CCC students were represented in the best fashion. They had filled those boxes with all those items and educational gifts. Above all, they filled their teacher's heart with so many acts of kindness that it melted the Russian's hearts. The former "evil empire," the very country that had robbed the sponsor of a peaceful, secure childhood, awaited his presence! What a challenge!

Each Russian teacher submitted a detailed request for who they wanted to visit their city. The American Councils ultimately made the final decision about where each of the American teachers would go. The teacher who would be matched with the Northwest sponsor was Dinara Zakhorove. The school was Gymnasium 9, Togliatti, Russia.

The two months prior to departure included medical briefings, inoculations, new clothes suitable for the Russian winter, and a passport/visa. The Shawnee Mission School District was most gracious in allowing the sabbatical. The real dilemma was finding a substitute for the CCC classes.

The class was familiar with one substitute who, by consensus, is one of the finest available in the district. She was familiar with the procedures of

the class. She readily agreed to take the classes but was uncomfo
so many students. It was suggested that the CCC students work
classroom during her tenure. This could not be done to the stu

Mike Meier, class president, stepped forward and assume
control. Mike's middle name was "volunteering." He was a na
leader and held the respect of both students and faculty. Grac
to be reported during the sponsor's absence. Mike was giver
to administer grades and Karen Miltko, the substitute, wou
stamp his decisions and also fill out computer grade forms.

Trust was always paramount in working with CCC studer
was time to put it to the ultimate test. There was never a c
garding the continuity or the quality of the CCC classes. Th
and teachers were not aware of the departure date. They w
told that one day there would be a substitute teacher at the
their idea of community service would be en route to Russia

In preparing to leave for the "evil empire," there were s
cerns about a safe return. Much of the literature from the
Councils wasn't even shared with the families of the teachers.
ings on what to do and how to act in public were all conti
CCC's beliefs. The American Councils was most helpful. E
scribing arrivals and safety assurances were sent home perioc

Before leaving Washington, D.C., the group was briefed o
ditions within Russia. The Russian literacy rate (99 percent) is
highest in the world. Two special problems plague the Russ
system: the rise of private schools with a charge for tuition ar
provision for "special education."

The concept of the family being required to pay tuition for
was absolutely foreign to them. Quality education had always
out cost. In the past, no one admitted the existence of student
cial needs. These "special kids" were simply hidden from vie

The plane trip to Russia seemed to last forever. The grou
proaching the largest nation on earth. On approach into M
port, the group became very quiet. The former group solic
denly vanished.

The next test would be acceptance of our passports coml
the retrieval of luggage. The group would learn firsthand if
any truth to the horror stories of travel to this part of the wo

one hoped that the Russians would not weigh their luggage. The additional gifts and provisions I had brought certainly took the bags beyond the maximum weight allowed.

The person ahead was asked to open her bags. The person behind was forced to pay $145 in overweight charges. All of her bags were searched and weighed. She was absolutely petrified. When she finally joined the group, the American Councils lodged a strong protest for her treatment. They discovered that the Russian customs officer had absconded with the $145! Welcome to Moscow!

Words cannot describe the feelings of being in that former Communist capital. The bus proceeded to the heart of Moscow. The hotel was not one anyone would have chosen. It was antiquated and moldy. It had no hot water. There was a shower over the tub but no shower curtain. The soap wouldn't foam up, and the towels were much too small for their intended purpose. The uncontrollable temperature was almost stifling.

At the Washington briefing, the group was informed that the Russian hotel system doesn't rent rooms to individuals. They rent beds. If there is an empty bed in your room, you might expect a visitor any hour of the day or night. Gender was not an issue. At exactly midnight, after an exciting concert at the Bolshoi Ballet, the phone rang. A woman's voice explained she was scheduled for the room. A few minutes later she called and asked for sex.

The phone was immediately pulled from the receiver. A refrigerator was propped in front of the door. The lady never appeared during a vigil that brought no sleep. A protest the following morning brought reassurance that it would never happen again. Sadly, they added that the only people in Moscow making any money were the prostitutes.

An interpreter finally arrived from Togliatti. She was a thirty-four-year-old woman who was married to a Russian soldier. Her English was perfect. No taxi was available to the train depot. She stood at the curb and hitchhiked a ride! Late that night, the train departed from Moscow.

Trains are the principal method of transportation in Russia and fares are cheap. Each compartment on the train accommodates four people. Attempting to exit the cabin for a restroom trip, I found a very large man standing directly in front of the compartment. He spoke in Russian. No words were exchanged, for the bathroom was priority one.

When the train arrived in Togliatti, the same man appear
the compartment, picked up the suitcases without speaking, a
train. "Welcome to Togliatti, it is an honor to have you in ou
carried the luggage to a waiting car, smiled, and left. His assig
been as a bodyguard for the American teacher.

Vitaly and Natalia Gopko are two of the most gracious p
could ever meet. They volunteered to host the visiting educ
English was poor and communication was facilitated throug
versal language of signs. Within five minutes, Vitaly went out
to explain that both he and his wife were atheists and asked if
any difference. Vitaly was a printer and Natalia had numerou
of which was teaching English. Unfortunately, few Russians h
portunity to speak English.

The current Russian financial system does not allow chech
tic" money. The American Councils provided $200 for the h
This seemed like an absolute fortune to them and it made m
possible.

The Gopkos had no car but had hired a driver. Upon arriv
nasium 9 looked every bit like a traditional American schoc
Russia, Ben Franklin would have spotted the traditional scl
Every student rose and remained standing as the guest te
pared materials ready for class. The roll was filled with tradit
sian names like Igor, Vladimir, Nicolai, Sergei, Irina, and M:
room was uncomfortably hot. The heat is turned on every yea
tain date whether it is needed or not. Speaking very slowly
sponsor said, "I am honored and surprised to be here." Hopin
derstood, his rate of speech remained painfully deliberate.

Suddenly, Igor raised his hand and said in perfect Englisl
(they call all their teachers by their first name), you may spe
Their knowledge of English was astounding! They soon spied
gifts and wanted anything made in the USA. From a Kansas C
store, there were "I am loved" buttons. They immediately pu
The cache of pencils, pictures, books, *anything American*, d
in short order. They also helped themselves to rolls of pennie

Now that the ice had been broken, they were informed
CCC. Most Russian children have no experience with religic
ity. The Russian teacher cautioned not to mention God unle

dents did. The concept of altruism was completely foreign. Speaking the words "the doer of good becomes good" in their native tongue meant nothing in translation!

It was appalling to hear that the teachers made a mere $25 a month, if they were paid at all. What could these children give to others when they had so little themselves?

The first lesson was to write an anonymous letter of appreciation to all of their teachers. The students were quick learners. They were genuinely interested in the CCC program. Their assignment that night was to do something that would make their parents' evening easier. Many of the students agreed to tell their parents that they loved them and appreciated all that they had sacrificed for their well-being.

The next step was to find students who were in need of tutoring. This was a sensitive area. The approach of the students was amazing. Often words like "thank you," "how are you?" "may I help you?" "take my chair," were heard. And so it began! As one of the students said, "Goodness is in the air!"

Every day there was a visit to a different school, a university, a nursery, and so forth. In each new place the seeds of the "doer of good becomes good" were planted. There were meetings with curriculum heads, presidents of universities, high school principals, assemblies, radio broadcasters, and their audiences.

There was a young man who sat through one class who, very reluctantly, asked if he could come again to the next hour. The response was the same as if in America: "If you can get out of your class, you can come in!" Sergei returned and again sat in the front row.

The purpose and mechanics of community service were conveyed again. When the bell rang, each student expressed individual thanks. Sergei was hesitant to leave. His eyes were extremely expressive and he seemed like he was in a daze. "Ronald, this is the greatest thing I have ever learned!" You can imagine the gratitude Sergei received, as well as a big hug! He wanted to say more but needed help to do so.

The interpreter explained that at first, he was scared. Sergei had believed the propaganda he had heard about Americans. Clutching an American pencil, a picture of the Kansas capitol, and a handful of pennies, he said something in his Russian voice no one else heard. He said ever so softly, as if he were unsure of the consequences, "God bless you,

Ronald, and all of America." The only Russian on the visit
God's blessings remains a special memory!

Each day was like a growing crescendo, as if community serv
leased the constraints on their very souls. Their capacity to lea
held back by a totalitarian state, was enlarged and encouraged.
of Russian students spoke, a classroom in 1992 came to mind.
phenomenon at Shawnee Mission Northwest High School
again: community service is like the discovery of a direction, a

These Russian students were reacting in an identical mar
would find a way to apply the "doer of good becomes good." I
that young people all over the world respond to trust by being tr

The final day at Gymnasium 9 had arrived. Melancholy w
the air. Students, teachers, and parents had been as accep
"American" as one of their own. Everyone wanted to come
America. The principal of the school asked for help in finding
ican man that she could marry. She, like everyone else, saw nc
herself in Russia. They seemed unwilling to try again with
government. They saw in their guest the embodiment of all th
in life: freedom and an opportunity to pursue their own drea

Their most common response to questions dealing with the
ernment was a simple, "We must wait and see." All of their life
had been made from the top down, whereas in democrac
made from the bottom up. They had little or no faith in thei
make important decisions about their own futures.

The CCC sponsor, with a very heavy heart, walked into t
rium. How quickly the time had sped away. So much more
done for them! The program that they had prepared strai
emotion from laughter to pathos. The students sang their l
played every musical instrument, and they even discussed th
good becomes good." Suddenly all the performers formed a st
and presented this American a plate of hot pancakes. The i
kept saying, "Thank them, Ronald, they are giving them to yo
is a Russian church called St. Nicholas "of all pancakes." Once
a guild of pancake makers. They had been so successful that
were sufficient to build that church. Hot pancakes became a
gifts to God. Communism had blighted the land, but it did not
the beautiful religious tradition embodied in this custom. Ev
down as if waiting for the final farewell.

The sponsor's presentation began with the familiar admonition that "a hundred years from now, no one will really care what kind of home or car we had, but that we were significant in the life of a child"! To the Russian students, a recitation of, "Let There Be Peace on Earth and Let It Begin with Me / With God as Our Father, Brothers All Are We."

Overcome with emotion, the humbled American began a strain of the Kansas state song. "Oh, give me a home, where the buffalo roam." Pavarotti could not have sung it better! "Where the deer and the antelope play . . ." The students joined in the singing and almost blew the roof off:

> Home, home on the range . . .
> and the skies are not cloudy all day!

At the very end a Russian woman, in a Russian school, walked to a Russian-made piano and played "America the Beautiful"! In tears, the CCC sponsor was almost unable to accept a plaque that, among other things, said: "We surely will use your motto: The doer of good becomes good! We now have a much better understanding of your nation." The memory of that afternoon will never fade. Eighty-three years of Communist tyranny was undone by that simple phrase.

Returning to Moscow the next day, Vitaly and Natalia each embraced their guest and gave a kiss goodbye. In tears, Natalia kept saying, "You are a very nice man, we will miss you!" Leaving them was one of the most difficult moments of the trip.

There had been so much Cold War baggage that now left this weary traveler almost "empty-handed." There was a newfound sense of pride in country. Hopefully, the concept of community service would help change their lives for the better. Indeed, they had suffered enough! Through tears, I realized my Russian adventure was over.

The American teachers returned to Moscow and eagerly shared experiences with one another. A Russian magazine requested an article on the CCC. It was published in the *Active School*. Hopefully, it became a catalyst for change.

One last experience in Russia was to see the body of Lenin in Red Square. Security was extremely tight. To view the life-like remains invoked the words of Woodrow Wilson: "Only fools resist God's providence."

The trip back to the United States was anticlimactic. The teachers pooled their experiences and felt a kind of euphoria from the completion

of an incredible journey. The American Councils conducted a
in its office and each teacher videotaped the salient featu
odyssey into what was no longer referred to as the "evil empii
   Returning to Shawnee Mission Northwest was an emotion
for all. Mike Meier had led CCC through new projects. They
lar Day for an urgent request from a charity. The class collec
one hundred pounds of candy for distribution at a Halloween
over two hundred children attending.
   Throughout this book, the need for schools to redefine *trus*
reiterated. Not one student had been truant during the tea
sence. Every CCC site reported no problems of any kind. The
teacher, Karen Miltko, reported that Mike had simply taken
reception at school, complete with refreshments, was a touch
to the goodness of Northwest's young people.
   There were many lessons learned on both sides of the Atla

1. Students can be trusted when given the opportunity.
2. Students care about what is important to them. They c
   care about the well-being of others.
3. Community service must be a part of every student's *daily*
4. Students are the same the world over; they need an opp
   grow in humanness. Community service is the mecha
   gives them the opportunity.
5. The American Councils had dubbed each of us a teacher
   This type of diplomacy has many benefits and certainly r
   both continued and expanded. It is one of the most effici
   taxpayers' money.
6. Totalitarian regimes ultimately cannot diminish a natio
   for free expression. Nearly eighty years of Communis
   had no lasting effect on these people!

   The CCC received a letter about a month after the retu
sponsor to the United States. It spoke volumes in a single pag
"Ronald, we are sorry for what we have done to the world."
   Rodgers and Hammerstein's song in *South Pacific* also s
umes about schools and students: "You've got to be careful
Prejudice and hatred are not qualities that come naturally
How true it is that children learn what they live!

If children live with criticism,
> They learn to condemn.

If children live with hostility
> They learn to fight.

If children live with fear,
> They learn to be apprehensive.

If children live with pity,
> They learn to feel sorry for themselves.

If children live with ridicule,
> They learn to be shy.

If children live with jealousy,
> They learn to feel envy.

If children live with encouragement,
> They learn confidence.

If children live with tolerance,
> They learn patience.

If children live with praise,
> They learn appreciation.

If children live with acceptance,
> They learn to love.

If children live with approval,
> They learn to like themselves.

If children live with sharing,
> They learn generosity.

If children live with recognition,
> They learn it is good to have a goal.

If children live with honesty,
> They learn truthfulness.

If children live with fairness,
> They learn justice.

If children live with kindness and consideration,
> They learn respect.

If children live with security,
> They learn to have faith in themselves and in those about them.

If children live with friendliness,
> They learn the world is a nice place in which to live.

(by Dorothy Law Nolte)

The doer of good becomes good! As a result of this simple message, we may all one day finally live in peace!

CHAPTER SUMMARY

1. The outstanding work of the CCC students came to th
   of the American Councils in Washington, D.C., and res
   invitation for the sponsor to share about CCC wit
   formed country in what was once the Soviet Union.
2. The concept of community service was unfamiliar to
   sentatives from Russia at the initial meeting in Del;
   many expressed an interest in learning about it anc
   shared with their schools.
3. Prior to my visit to Russia, I had reexamined my pre
   perceptions of Russia based on the Cold War's vers
   "evil empire."
4. My CCC students continued in my absence to be trust\
   competent, initiating some projects on their own and t
   of others.
5. I learned prior to going to Russia that Russians were l
   cated and were not comfortable with private schools ai
   education."
6. When I was in Russia it was apparent that the coun
   transition and that a strong criminal element was em‹
   seeking total control of that country. I was sent to Tog
   sia, which is a heavily industrialized city of nearly o
   people who are employed mainly in the Russian car m
   ing industry.
7. Almost all travel in Russia is by train, which is prec
   dangerous. My trips were uneventful but frightening a
   dividuals as "bodyguards."
8. I stayed with a Russian couple whose two boys were ;
   the university. The Americans gave me $200 to give th
   was a great amount to them.
9. I found the Russian students to be no different than tl
   ican counterparts, although they expressed a greater
   community service.
10. The motto of the CCC was accepted completely anc
    tionally by the Russian school, Gymnasium 9.

11. The Russian students and teachers adopted community service as a permanent adjunct to their education, with one teacher thinking it would help alleviate drug problems among their youth.

12. Nearly all the students I came in contact with, and many of their teachers, expressed a desire to leave Russia and come to America. It seems as if they had experienced enough suffering and wanted to start over in America.

13. A summary of the CCC program was published in a Russian publication, the *Active School,* and will possibly become part of the Russian school curriculum.

14. This experienced proved to me that community service and the CCC model could be transplanted even into a foreign country. *Trust* and *love* seem to be universal as proven by my experience there, giving hope that ultimately we *can* live in peace.

7

THE FUTURE

I don't know what your destiny will be, but one thing I do know: the only ones among you who will be really happy are those who have sought and found how to serve.

—Albert Schweitzer

Ten years is a very short period of time. However, in that time period, change has become the norm in all aspects of our society. Today, we see such changes as cloning, embryos for sale, professional baby-raisers, electronic stores, debit cards, computerized education, and a multitude of others too numerous to list. It is up to today's teachers to prepare our students for a future that will be new to us all.

High school world history students are sending e-mail messages to the most remote areas on earth. Commercial space travel will soon be able to circumvent the globe. Field trips could possibly become "country trips."

The voyage to Russia was so frustrating due to the inability to communicate. We have lost so much by our lack of interpersonal skills.

What is the future of the CCC or of community service? Community service will always remain a major part of my students' lives. We like to say, "Once a CCC member, always a CCC member!" No matter how great the scientific advancements, human beings will forever need one another.

Tom Hanks taught us something in his portrayal of the str:
son in the movie *Castaway*. The lesson was a simple one inde
all social by nature. If the Rene Spitz study would be conduc
even two hundred years from now, the results would be
Marasmus! Without socialization, we die. Victoria Secun
would also remain the same. Young people will turn out to l
where there is adult involvement in their lives!

Why did Woodrow Wilson say, "There is no higher religio
man service"? He understood human nature. Even as pre
daily life was marked by acts of kindness. Today, Colin Powe
us to likewise volunteer and to give of ourselves in acts of kin
state of Kansas has begun a movement that will ensure its yo
an exposure to community service. House Bill 2352, author
Benlon and passed by the Kansas legislature, requires that ev
school in the state offer community service in its curriculum.

Northwest High School CCC had an inconspicuous begi
only seventeen students, but notice how quickly that swell
four hundred! Once offered, community service will grow. I
ture of the class. For years we have been saying, "One goo
serves another." Now we will see that one good turn creat
Even now, former students who have been members of the (
or visit to share that they have continued their service to oth

For example, Stephanie Nash, a former CCC student, still
a random act of kindness every day. She has the sign, "Th
Good Becomes Good" taped to her computer. Adam Benlon
week at college, returned home to get appliances for a poor
he "found" near the college. One more student returned from
share that the CCC brought him out of almost eight years of c
during which he thought of killing himself every night! All of
students know that "my *worst* day is someone's *best* day"!

Many times teachers ask, "What's going to happen to tl
CCC once their sponsor retires?" It should be very obviou
sponsor has a great deal of trust in young people. The numl
program are growing, certainly not because of the program it
students see or hear about the many acts of kindness that st
doing and how pleased they are with the program. Some stu
this class for four semesters and progressively do more each

The student president designs the entire year and picks the entire executive board. This was a new experience for a veteran teacher. It is difficult to relinquish a substantive role for a procedural one. For ten years it has worked well. There is every assurance that it will continue with the high quality standard that students set for themselves.

The community itself has a tremendous stake in the continued existence of this program. Like a "textbook," the elementary schools will have an increased need for tutors. Today's senior adults will populate our numerous retirement villages. Teachers are the most altruistic people in our society and any new teacher/sponsor will bring new programs and fresh opportunities to these places of need.

Like most states, Kansas is experiencing a money shortage with serious consequences for the public schools. The Northwest library fund had been cut from $26,000 to a mere $5,000 for the coming school year. Upon hearing this, CCC students immediately started to brainstorm ways to make up the funds. Before the current school year ended, the CCC had replaced all the magazine subscriptions that had cancelled due to lack of money.

Other choice projects are in the making so that our educational program will continue at the same level. Look at some of the testimonials from students, parents, legislators, and community individuals in this book. They represent a strength that will be here for a long, long time. Once you begin a class like the CCC, there will be no turning back. Resources will never diminish! Ten years ago it was a leap of faith. Ten years later, it is simply a leap forward.

A COMMENTARY BY THE AUTHOR

As I near the end of my career, I find that each new school year is a bonus. It seems only natural to issue a profound commentary on forty years in education. I have been blessed with excellent, highly motivated students. I said earlier that at one time there was only one influential institution: the family. All of man's needs were met through that single source.

My early life was deeply affected by someone for whom family was his entire existence. Born in a small village in Germany, which was totally destroyed in two world wars, prejudice denied this highly gift(cess to formal education. Consequently, my father left behinc no letters, and no profound artistic works of any kind.

This "man in overalls" roamed the streets and alleys of my delivering the mail to the town's bedridden. He distributed g the hungry. When offering neighbors a ride to town on a c(shoveling tall snow drifts, he never asked for anything in reti was its own reward for him!

Unable to read, he put three sons through high school ai He possessed self-made skills that schools could only hope t(He was at times quiet, but often played his accordion so ot dance and have a good time. For the moment, one could forg dens of life. He never complained other than that he alway: Lincoln Continental! It always remained a dream.

When he died, the *entire* town came to his funeral. Each p(to outdo the other with stories of the kindness my father l them. They would never see his kind again. When the wea most formally educated man in my hometown went to his passing went unnoticed and unmourned. What a pity! Wha My father would have loved the motto of the CCC: the doer (comes good! He is dearly missed.

> There is a Law that man should love his neighbor as himself. Ir
> hundred years it should be as natural as breathing or the u
> gait; but if he does not learn it he must perish.
>
> —Alfred

I am the CCC president for the 2002–2003 school year. On the (chosen, my heart was racing, my palms were sweating, and I w cited! Where am I going with the CCC? I want to turn this prog a volunteer program that supports its school and community. I \ fundraise and most importantly, to give. I think no matter how : brought to volunteerism, you should be respected. At the same best recognition possible should be given to you. And the best re(possible is the look of appreciation on the face of the person : helped. I want to bring the CCC to the point of friendship, kindr erosity, and love.

I want people to feel good about themselves when they leave this class. I want every person to walk into life and feel the same love and comradeship with every person they meet. I want to help one person meet the grandfather they never had, at Lakeview. I want one person to meet the little brother they may never have had, at Nieman Elementary School. And I want one person to realize how much more they can give. If I can do that, I will feel successful as president of CCC and walk away from the program more fulfilled than ever imaginable.

—Miranda Flener, President, 2002–2003 school year

Appendix A

COMMUNITY COMMENTS

Always do right. This will gratify some people and astonish the rest.

—Mark Twain

During the past ten years, the Shawnee, Kansas, community has responded with a plethora of support letters, letters of appreciation, as well as numerous awards and scholarships for the CCC. Expressions of support have come from the White House. The Kansas governor and his wife, who have also visited Shawnee Mission Northwest, have lent their enthusiastic support to the CCC and the students.

One of the most common remarks I have heard from the community is the overwhelming disbelief that high school students would even be interested in community service. So many have said that they have totally misunderstood today's adolescents and that they are simply amazed at their trust level. Some even went so far as to say that crucial bond issues were passed because of the CCC.

In this section, I have included a few sample comments from the hundreds of people who have written me over the past ten years. The number of community expressions of support from over the years fills several boxes! It is safe to say that the image of "sex, drugs, and rock and roll" is a thing of the past. Candidates for local office have sought endorsement from the CCC and several candidates have had their pictures

taken working side-by-side with CCC members. There have
many newspaper articles covering the CCC's activities and
nesses have shown their support by donating food and mercl
many of the activities. The impact on community service was ¡
the state legislation voted that community service must be i
all accredited Kansas schools in the fall of 2002. This primer i
to be a guide to those school districts who search for guidanc(
this state mandate. I believe that my students are typical o
group and that the "sleeping giant" is awake, and I doubt if h
sleep again!

It has been difficult to choose these comments of support
that the ones that follow will convey the community's feeling:
CCC and its quite phenomenal students.

Henry Floyd Brown has a unique reputation. According t(
Kansas Secretary of Corrections: "Henry is the most dangerou
ning criminal to ever occupy a cell in the 110-year history of ¡
State Prison." I had known Henry for several years prior to
and received the following in a letter as he contemplated his

> Now that I am really close to getting out . . . it is a scary feeling t(
> self walking out like the day I was born except now, no one will
> to take care of me until I learn to walk. . . . I want to be a pı
> member of society. Will they help me? . . . no gifts, just a job wh
> earn my way at a living wage. I have *nothing*. I am worse off than ¡
> who floats up out of the sea. There are programs and loans to
> refugee, but there are no programs to help the ex-con. No doubt
> food stamps, but where will I cook the food? In the past, I jus
> something . . . but I have no intention of doing that this time . .
> of your classes. Maybe they will have some ideas.
>
> —Love and peace, Kansas State Pris

For the past five years, Henry has been a "member" of the
dents invite him to dinners and parties and have given him tl
things to make his reentry to society easier. At seventy-five yє
with no social security and no savings, these students have sav
payers of Kansas at least $250,000 by enabling Henry to ¡
prison. More important, they have rescued someone who
could save. They did it with friendship! Read on to see how
affected other community members:

Dear Members of the CCC . . . You are truly wonderful, caring and impressive people! The Volunteer Services Department, Visiting Nurse Services, our staff, and most importantly, our patients, thank you for your very generous donation. We realize that this grand check means many hours of hard work and a "Dollar Day" at school. Please know we appreciate the opportunity you give us to be able to help our patients. Do not underestimate the importance of your gift.

—B. Lucinda Eppard, Manager,
Volunteer Services Department, Visiting Nurse Association

I feel compelled to write you and thank you. . . . Thank you for your dream, which Cougars Community Commitment stands for. Mr. Poplau, simply put, I was blown away by the students' willingness to help and touched by their goodness. . . . What sets me apart is the fact that I know that the Doer of Good Becomes Good.

—John Duckworth, community resident

On behalf of the board and staff of AYS, and more importantly, the youth and families who enter AYS's doors, I extend my heartfelt gratitude. None of our services would be possible without involved and committed people like the CCC students.

—Dennis Vanderpool, CEO, Associated Youth Services

We have cleaned yards for the elderly and the handicapped. We have cleaned streams and parks and highways. We have provided delightful food and dances in intergenerational programs. We have moved people and storage to people. We have painted and painted. We have offered Hallowe'en and Christmas parties for twelve years to the community children. Toys and food have been collected and distributed to children in the metropolitan area.

Week after week, students help stock and sort to assist in garage sale efforts to help in the purchase of our building. Our organization has benefited greatly through having an annual crop of youth to volunteer talent, resources and strength to help the less fortunate.

—Evelyn VanKernseke, President/CEO,
Shawnee Community Services

Without CCC student support and reliability to our students with disabilities we could not have smoothly handled many situations. CCC, in my opinion, teaches one of the most valuable lessons life has to offer, that [of]

. . . being of service to another fellow human being and getting
ing of satisfaction that only comes from selfless giving.

—Mark Scott, Transition S
SMNW High School "Job C

Once again your Cougars Committed to Community students ha
through with assistance in the cleanup of a property for one of S
citizens. . . . Our thanks go out to your program and students, tl
make a difference!

—Ken Doresky, AICP Neighborhood Planner, City of

When Ron Poplau talked to me about his CCC students' nursi
visits and the many lonely residents, a new writing idea evolved
my freshmen students wrote letters to the residents and eagerly
responses. By the end of the school year, some of the students
dents had become regular correspondents. I appreciate Ron and
classes for making this possible for my students. It was rewarding
young and old.

—Kay Kasse
Language Arts Department, SMNW Hig

I wanted to personally thank you for the wonderful communit
program that you have developed and directed at Shawnee
Northwest High School. I know that my grandmother looked fc
the weekly visits and time spent with her by your students. M
mother and I often visited about the politeness and interest tl
people extended towards her and all the residents of Lakeview.

—Al C. Overton, relative, Lakeview Village

I just wanted to thank you for all your efforts toward making heal
give to the needy families. Without the help of the CCC we w
have been able to provide so many families with necessary hygie

—Laura Baack, St. Luke's Lutherai

I would like to thank the CCC program at SMNW High Schoo
viding a student fourth period as a peer for Jessica, a disabled st
a wheelchair. You have no idea [the] . . . joy Ashley brought to Jes:
I can't say enough good things about this program.

—Vicki Penny, Parapro
Special Education Department, SMNW Hig

When children grow up in an affluent suburb, they don't always get the chance to really help others less fortunate than themselves, or have contact with children and seniors who have needs that can't be addressed through social services. I don't just mean raising money through some school drive, I mean actual physical and emotional contact with people who change you, by just allowing you to assist them in some real sense.

Your class gave my daughter that opportunity and she has said many times that it was the best lesson of her high school career. She learned that giving is more rewarding than wanting and that she had many gifts within her to share with others. I wish that every high school in this country offered this program and that it was a requirement for graduation. We teach many things these days other than reading, writing, math, and the sciences. I wish we didn't neglect to allow the soul to teach itself.

—Libbie Cole, parent of ex-CCC student, Shawnee, Kansas

My classes and I have worked with the CCC in several projects over the years. Each project has always resulted in positive experiences for my students and for the CCC students. One of our projects included the mixing and baking of cakes for children of the homeless. Another connected me with a lady from a retirement home that prepared an Italian meal for my International Foods class. Not only did she share her ethnic cooking information and skills, but also her family experiences as a child. Students enjoyed having her and gained a new appreciation for the elderly. My students and I enjoy helping the CCC whenever possible.

—Bonnie Salazar, Foods Teacher, SMNW High School

Dear Mr. President: . . . the Cougars Community Commitment program at Shawnee Mission Northwest High School is unique in the nation and was designed to encourage and support student involvement in worthwhile community service. Students enrolled in the program are graded on their commitment and participation in community service. This award-winning program, with over 50 percent of the junior and senior classes participating, has proven to be very successful for the students and the community. Students of all physical and mental abilities learn the value and self-esteem of contributing to their community. Their activities include tutoring elementary students, holding monthly parties at the high school for senior citizens, working with drug addicts and convicts, and providing Thanksgiving and Christmas meals for the needy. They contribute hours of community service and their own money to a variety of projects that benefit those less fortunate than themselves. . . . I believe that the student participation in

this community program is the "unsung" story of the majori
young people in this nation.

—Dennis Moore, Member of (
U.S. House of Representatives, Washingt

I want to tell you how the CCC impacted my life. Struggling thr
ing a teenager and my parents' divorce, the CCC allowed me th
tunity to shine in a positive light. This class is one that taught me
"real world" had to offer. It was a sense of reality to visit the
Community Center every day and see people that struggled for
day. Visiting the nursing homes showed me that I had a lot to lea
what life had to offer. The children at the elementary schools gav
portunity to change the world. This was the class that I looked fo
every day. It was a great way to get involved in the community
friends and I really felt like we made a difference in the commu

—Stephanie Nash, Program Representative, Baker L

Megan had always done well in school and enjoyed several goo
ships. Once we moved from our home of many years to the Shaw
sion Northwest High School area, she experienced difficulties
and making friendships and we even feared that she was suicida
also began to gain weight and her grades began to decline. . . .'
CCC came along and Megan became involved. Suddenly,
changed. She couldn't get enough of this class. She darted out th
go to the nursing home, the community center that supplied fo
needy, and many other places. In her second year at SMNW, M
president of the CCC. She worked hard to support existing en
and identify new needs in the community. She was awarded seve
arships for her service and honors for her role as a student leader
Today, Megan continues to serve her community as a teacher o
toddlers, and preschoolers with disabilities. She looks back on he
ment period as one that led to new skills, increased awareness of
strengths that continue to serve her as an adult.

—Kathy Davis, mother of a former CCC |

There are few, if any, higher-level classes that I had found before
that taught anything as life-changing as CCC. The lessons of con
philanthropy, and the basic quality of all humanity regardless of a
or socioeconomic status come from experiences that the studen

teer themselves for, not a lecture or book. CCC opens the heart as well as the mind, and shows students that they can impact someone's life for the better. Though that one semester of my life is over, I still visit my adopted "grandparent" and use the lessons the CCC has taught me every day in dealing with every person around me, and as a past member of the CCC I will always carry the motto and core of CCC into my life forever: The Doer of Good Becomes Good.

—Shannon Marsh, National Merit Scholar, SMNW High School

I am writing from a unique perspective about Ron Poplau and the CCC as I probably was closely involved with the precursors of this organization. At least, I and my two sons were certainly recipients of the goodness and love that was inherent in its formation and continued success.

I first met Ron in 1979, in the basement of a local school when I went with one of my oldest son's junior high school teachers to present about being the single parent of two boys with muscular dystrophy. He came up afterward and asked me to present at his sociology class segment on death and dying. I agreed and did so up until several years ago. One of the most difficult things I ever had to do was present to one of Ron's classes with my oldest son sitting at the front of the room only months before he died. I do believe that the success and worth of the CCC is due to the student involvement and commitment, but Ron Poplau is nothing if not the issue of his father, and the impetus and core of the CCC.

There are too many examples of his kindness and too little space here to mention them all, but the key things include: organizing a "Byron Grosko Day" for my son at the end of his junior year and honoring him by giving him a computer keyboard that was purchased with funds donated by Ron's sociology students; helping to organize a horde of strong male students to come to our home early in the morning to help lift the boys after I had back surgery; constant support and friendship for Byron and myself from Ron, when he was hospitalized eight times in the last nine months of his senior year and his life; helping Byron, through the sociology class on death and dying, to plan his own funeral at age sixteen, and when the time came, preparing the music that Byron had chosen in these plans and giving the eulogy for him at a funeral that was attended by over four hundred students from Byron's beloved Northwest.

But it didn't stop there, for Byron's younger brother, began his dying process only two short years after, and he didn't have the opportunity to be in Ron's sociology class in order to plan his funeral. But when it seems apparent that Sean was weakening and close to the end of his sophomore year,

and based upon something I said about the desire he had to go t‹
place with an ocean, preferably Hawaii, Ron and his students, a₁
from Northwest and the Shawnee community arranged for Sean
friend, and me to go to Hawaii for a week. We had a marvelous
even sent a crate of pineapples to the school in gratitude for their l
   Two days after we returned form Hawaii, Sean died at the a
Ironically, the pineapples arrived at the school on that day. Ron o₁
did the eulogy, this time for Sean. All of these caring and helpí
were provided by Ronald SMNW prior to the CCC class! Late₁
recipient of a CCC teddy bear their first Christmas and the stu
on the living room floor and sang carols to me. A few years later
dent helped me with serving Thanksgiving dinner for persons wi
their families, and other needy individuals. The next year, so
brought their parents and siblings to help! Ron Poplau is a hun
and is uncomfortable with accolades that address his unending g
of spirit and kindness toward his fellow man. I am taking this op₁
to say that he is the force and heart of the CCC and he has mad‹
of difference in my life and many others.

                                              —Joyce Grosko, form‹

Appendix B

AWARDS

Nothing Succeeds Like Success.

—Alexander Dumas the Elder

PENNEY'S GOLDEN RULE AWARD

The class was awarded this the first year of existence. In the ensuing years, four individual students won the award. One judge remarked to the sponsor: "We just assumed you would have someone in the running each year!"

THE KANSAS CITY *STAR*

The *Star* embarked on a journalistic feat that won local, state, and national awards. They chose twelve area programs that represented twelve different virtues essential to young people. Shiril Kaspar, a *Star* reporter, considered the CCC to represent compassion. She articulated skepticism about a group of high school students meriting inclusion into such a prestigious newspaper series titled "Raising Kansas City."

She frequented every community site for several months. V
tendance, one of Northwest's students committed suicide.
the family and school were devastated. Nearly the entire
tended the funeral. At Christmas, the CCC invited families
that had sustained a loss. The reporter attended this special
Each family was given a teddy bear, representative of the ‹
concern expressed by the CCC. The CCC sang carols and
family a positive memory about the person who was lost.

Upon the conclusion of the ceremony, any leftover refreshn
given to the reporter to share with her colleagues. On the w
the newspaper, Ms. Kaspar came across a homeless man b
food. She gave him the cookies. She phoned the class and sha
perience of giving and reminisced about the students and the
concern! "You are so right," she said. "The Doer of Good
Good! I will write your story!"

HABITAT II AWARD

The city of Shawnee nominated the CCC for one of the top
programs in the country. A summary of the program, prepare
resentative of Kansas University, was sent to an international ‹
on volunteerism in Istanbul, Turkey.

SPIRIT OF GIVING AWARD

One of the most touching awards came from Bill Graves, g
Kansas. The governor and his wife visited Northwest on tw
occasions. The CCC gathered in the Topeka Capitol Rotunda
this award. The Kansas State Prison Inmate Choir performed
that the students had provided Christmas gifts for the inmate
the choir sang their hearts out! Needless to say, we all shed t

SCHOOL OF SERVICE AWARD

For three years in a row, Shawnee Mission Northwest
named a "School of Service" by the National Youth Alliance. ‹
two students each year were given $1,000 scholarships.

CCC DAY

The city of Shawnee on two separate occasions, designated a day for the CCC throughout the city. They presented the class with keys to the city.

Other awards include: Shawnee Optimists Scholarships and Awards, Sertoma, La Sertoma (local, regional, and international awards), Newcomer's Symbol of Caring, Knights of Columbus, Lion's Club, and Cards for Kansas City.

These awards convince the students of the importance of the work they do for others. These students do "ordinary" things but in an "extraordinary" manner. Candidates for city office in Shawnee chose to begin their campaign for office by appearing before the CCC seeking the class's support.

In the long run, the real awards are the number of lives, both young and old, that are changed by the efforts of the students. Ten years after the program began, many of the former students visit or keep in touch. They always mention the effect the program had on their lives. They never fail to mention that "The Doer of Good Becomes Good."

Appendix C

FORMS

$\mathbf{W}$e live, unfortunately, in a society inundated with legalities. For ten years, these forms have served us well and cover almost any eventuality. In most cases, permission requires three signatures: the student, sponsor, and the parents. To date, there have been no legal difficulties due to the use of these forms.

Disclaimer: please allow your building administration and district legal personnel to approve appropriate forms for your needs. You may copy any material from these forms that is necessary. The forms in this book are not intended for individual school or district use. They are merely what has worked for the CCC and are intended to be a guide/ example.

CCC Introduction Form

Name _____ _____ Junior   _____ :

I. What kind of car do you have? _____

2. Do you have or do you have access to a truck of any kind? _____

3. Please list your hobbies: _____

_____

4. Do you have a job? _____

    A. Where do you work? _____

    B. Hours a week? _____

    C. What time do you have to be at work each day? _____

5. WEEKENDS: Are you available for projects on weekends especially Saturday

_____

6. Do you have a special interest: cars, movies, music, etc.? _____

_____

7. Based on your interests, other students' comments, etc., what kind of servic
    especially interested in?

_____ Tutoring   _____ Lawn care   _____ Working with delinquents

_____ Working with elderly   _____ Animal care   _____ Community C

8. How do you rate yourself as a conversationalist with adults? _____

_____

9. Do you like to do any of the following:

_____ fish _____ dance _____ sing _____ play pool _____ play cards _____ crafts

10. Do you consider yourself good with tools? Can you help someone with light carpentry work or fix minor things on a car? Explain:

_____

_____

_____

_____

11. Are you willing to carpool and/or take someone (another student) in your car if needed?

(emergencies, etc.) _____

12. Can you bring any of the following:

_____ food _____ clothing _____ money _____ homemade desserts

13. Would you like to tutor in math or computers to elementary students?

_____ Yes _____ No

14. Is there a special interest you have, e.g., helping with MS projects, cancer causes, children with disabilities, etc.?

_____

15. Why did you take this class? Please be specific and provide as much information as you can. Thanks.

CCC   Name _____

                                      Hour _____

OFF CAMPUS PARENTAL PERMISSION FORM

The Shawnee Mission School District offers a number of courses and activities wl
classroom, instruction and community work experience, observations, and |
Courses which require community based experiences are biology 2H, Consorti
Childhood I and II, Fashion Careers II, Health Careers, Advanced Journalism, Mai
tion II, Business Technology II, Radio and TV Production, ROTC, Sociology II, U.
Yearbook, International Languages, classes taught at other Shawnee Mission sch
nity college classes, Cougars Community Commitment, PACE courses, some spe
and vocational classes.

REQEST FOR SPECIAL ENROLLMENT

Name _____

Student # _____

I/we, the parents of the above named student, request that he/she be permitted
in these courses and/or activities for the 2003–2004 school year. I/We have read
formation provided by the school at the time of enrollment and agree to the ‹
participation. I/We understand that the Shawnee Mission School District doe
transportation for enrolled students and that no insurance of any sort is provide
participating in courses with community work experience, observation, or perfc
ities. For those students going to vocational training classes off the Northwest ‹
the district provides busing, it is strongly recommended that the student ride th
location. If they choose not to ride the bus, the school will not provide transpc
surance to participate in this program. My/Our signatures below indicate that I/v
and approve the enrollment and participation of our student in the above name
are willing to assume the responsibilities and risks in participation. **NOTE: TI
open lunch permit.**

Parent Signature _____   **Date** _____

Dear Parent/Guardian:

You probably already signed a Code 6 form when your child enrolled at Northw‹
to know what this form means in my CCC class.

   1. Your child will drive his/her car every day to his/her community service lo
   2. Your child may carpool with another student and can ride in a car driven by an
   3. Any accident is covered by your child's insurance.
   4. It is my expectation that all of my students will observe all driving and traff

If you have any questions, please feel free to contact me at (phone number).

Ronald W. Poplau

COUGARS COMMUNITY COMMITMENT
Shawnee Mission Northwest High School

Tutor Evaluation Form

Student's Name _____

Hour _____

Teacher's Name _____

School _____

This student has been working with you and your class during this semester. It is now your privilege to evaluate this student's performance. Please do so as thoroughly as possible and I appreciate your efforts on behalf of this student and our CCC program.

1. Was this student helpful and cooperative? _____

2. Was this student courteous? _____

3. How was this student's attendance? _____

_____

4. What letter grade would you give this student?   A   B   C   D   F

5. Would you want this student back again? _____

6. Would you take another CCC student during the next semester? _____

Comments: _____

_____

_____

Please give this form to your office and I will pick it up personally. Thank you for your involvement in the program.

R.W. Poplau

COUGARS COMMUNITY COMMITMENT

CCC Contract

Name _____

Hour _____

Cougars Community Commitment offers both you, the student, and the membe
community a meaningful, mutual experience in life. Trust and caring are the key fa
ing this class successful. As a member of this class, you agree to abide by the fol
tions:

1. To go to your daily commitment as quickly as possible. Arrange transportat
   of your activity.
2. To give genuine, caring service to each person in need (i.e., to apply your be
   tinually).
3. You are permitted only five absences. After five, you must make them up.
4. To abide by all regulations of the person, institution, or group you are assi
5. Grades are determined by attendance and the number of hours of comr
   given each quarter. Your performance may also be critiqued by whomeve
   Quality is of utmost importance.
6. Inform the sponsor when you will not be in class before your hour. A sub
   found to perform your service if your report is timely. Reliability is of grea
7. One truancy will result in the student being dropped from this class. This is absol
   limitations. Even if the truancy during the final days of the quarter or semester, ;
   be dropped from the class with loss of all credit.
8. If a misunderstanding occurs between the student and the person/place t
   is giving service, the matter will resolved by a meeting with the person, stui
   sponsor.

There are many scholarships and awards based on community service. Your inp
and suggestions are always welcome. Remember always

The doer of good becomes good!

Student Signature _____   Parent/Guardian Signature _____

Sponsor _____   Date _____

COUGARS COMMUNITY CHRONICLE

Vol. 2
September 3, 2003

We are off to an excellent start. All of you have a placement—we did it! We will be "in house" on Monday, September 8th. At that time you can decide if the site you are going to is what you want to do on an extended basis. Be sure to tell your site that you will not be there on Monday the 8th.

Hours and Requests

1. Carnival workers: We have a request from a school for students for Saturday, September 20th from 10:30 to 3:30.
2. Celebration Church: They would like to have three students each Sunday evening from 6:45 to 9:30 P.M. to babysit while the parents attend Bible class.
3. Parents Group: Babysitters are needed while parents attend meetings. First date is in October.
4. Safe Home: We will provide a pizza dinner at Safe Home. The CCC will buy sufficient pizza for the women and their children. We need desserts: cookies, cakes, etc. If you will bring homemade cookies you will receive one hour of credit for each dozen. You can bring as many as you like. We can always store them for later meals.
5. Pop can tabs: Continue to save these for Ronald McDonald House. One sandwich bag will give you one hour of credit.
6. Food: There is always a standing request for food. The number of families needing food increases every day. One case (24 cans) will give you three hours credit. Aldi is the least expensive place.
7. Clothing: You can bring bags of clothes any time. We plan on a garage sale later in the semester. Shawnee Community Center gives clothing away free every day to needy families.

REFERENCES

French, Scott. 1993. *Just This Once*. New York: Carol Publishing Group.

Fried, SuEllen, and Paula Fried. 1996. *Bullies and Victims*. New York: M. Evans.

Fried, SuEllen, and Paula Fried. 2003. *Bullies: Targets and Witnesses*. New York: M. Evans.

Glueck, Sheldon, and Eleanor Glueck. 1952. *Delinquents in the Making*. New York: Harper and Row.

Putnam, Robert D. 2000. *Bowling Alone*. New York: Simon and Schuster.

Reich, Charles A. 1970. *The Greening of America*. New York: Random House.

Secunda, Victoria. 1984. *By Youth Possessed*. New York: Bobbs Merrill.

Sorokin, Pitirim A. 1964. *The Basic Trends of Our Times*. New Haven, Conn.: College and University Press.

Spitz, Rene. 1945. "Hospitalism." In *Psychoanalytical Study of the Child*, Vol. 1 (pp. 53–74). New York: International Universities Press.

Toffler, Alvin. 1970. *Future Shock*. New York: Random House.

"Why Young People 'Go Bad.'" 1965. Interview with Sheldon and Eleanore Gluck. *U.S. News and World Report* (April 26): 56–62.

INDEX

ABOUT THE AUTHOR

Ronald W. Poplau has been in the field of education for forty-two years, and for the past ten years has witnessed literally thousands of students dramatically changed by community service classes. He is a member of the National Teachers Hall of Fame and also the Mid-America Education Hall of Fame.

Poplau resides in the Midwest, where his son and daughter are also professional educators in Blue Ribbon Schools of Excellence. Poplau continues his personal involvement in community service by assisting convicts to reenter society and feeding the homeless. He and his wife are also actively committed to wildlife preservation.